Praise for Marathon Wisdom

"I found Mara's book very enjoyable probably because with a similar running career, I resonated with her practical and wise insights. I will definitely recommend this book to my friends because of the way Mara honestly and openly tackles the problems that distance runners face and reveals how she tackled them. This is different from most other athletics books, which are usually autobiographies or coaching manuals. Congratulations!"

—Joyce Smith MBF, women's marathon pioneer and icon, two-time Olympian, former 3,000m world record-holder, winner of the first two London marathons and Tokyo marathons

....

"As an athlete, Mara left no stone unturned to get the best out of herself. By her own admission, she was a late starter and made mistakes along the way, but it should not be forgotten that Mara became one of Britain's most successful marathon runners. Her book, which looks back at her career, gives us great insights into what she got right and what she knows she could have done better. Each insight can be appreciated as a standalone or as part of a step-by-step journey through the joys and challenges of being a runner. Her book is full of practical down-to-earth advice for every level of runner, providing the right amount of guidance without being too detailed. I love the mix of her UK and Japanese experience, which will appeal to a wide audience. Overall, it is a great book for thinking positively and achieving more from running."

—Richard Nerurkar MBE, British former elite marathon runner, winner of 1993 World Cup Marathon, fifth in the 1996 Olympic Marathon, co-founder of the Great Ethiopian Run and author of Marathon Running: From Beginner to Elite

....

"I love the structure of Mara's first book, with the 42.195 insights making a strong framework for her engaging narrative. With the growing popularity of running, Mara's highly readable text will appeal to a global audience of runners from recreational through to elite level athletes. Her excellent points will also resonate with those outside the sport who are working towards professional and recreational goals of all kinds. Indeed, as an educator and an artist, I have already successfully drawn upon her ideas in my own work. I will certainly be recommending this book to colleagues, friends and family."

—Emma Coleman-Jones, senior schoolteacher, artist and fellow long-distance runner

....

To my parents, Dorothy and Norman, and to Shige.
Without their help I would never have realised my dream
of becoming a world-class athlete.

Mara Yamauchi

Marathon Wisdom

An Elite Athlete's Insights on Running and Life

Foreword by Jo Pavey

Meyer & Meyer Sport

British Library of Cataloguing in Publication Data

A catalogue record for this book is available from the British Library

Marathon Wisdom

Maidenhead: Meyer & Meyer Sport (UK) Ltd., 2022

ISBN: 978-1-78255-245-1

© 2022 by Meyer & Meyer Sport (UK) Ltd.

Aachen, Auckland, Beirut, Cairo, Cape Town, Dubai, Hägendorf, Hong Kong, Indianapolis, Maidenhead, Manila, New Delhi, Singapore, Sydney, Tehran, Vienna

 Member of the World Sport Publishers' Association (WSPA), www.w-s-p-a.org

Printed by Print Consult GmbH, Munich, Germany

Printed in Slovakia

ISBN: 978-1-78255-245-1

Email: info@m-m-sports.com

www.thesportspublisher.com

Contents

Foreword

Running a marathon is a massive challenge. It requires hours of tough training and unbelievable mental strength and you definitely have to put your heart and soul into it! The preparation phase through to running the event is as much of an emotional and mental battle, as a physical one. Completing a marathon is undoubtedly a great accomplishment, but so few people have actually reached the truly, world class performances that Mara achieved in her career, particularly as a clean athlete.

As a fellow distance runner, I feel very fortunate and privileged to have been a teammate of Mara's at many championships and to have stayed in contact with her after she finished competing. I always admired her steely determination and diligence to leave no stone unturned in pursuit of marathon success. I have strong memories of seeing Mara clipping along, totally focused, around the roads near Richmond Park in London. Shige was always on the bike helping her to keep precisely on target pace. She has always displayed such professionalism and dedication and has also fought back bravely from career-threatening injuries.

In her book, Mara shares an immense wisdom gained through running and dealing with life's challenges during her illustrious marathon career. She also honestly and bravely documents her mental health struggles, particularly after retirement from competition. This makes her achievements as an athlete, and in retirement as a coach, writer and commentator, even more admirable and the hope she speaks of is truly inspiring.

The reader is given many valuable insights about important issues in marathon running, including: mastering goal setting; building mental strength; executing performance; and reflecting on performance to make improvements. Mara stresses the importance of recovery, looking after yourself and being kind to yourself. She touches on the fascinating world of marathon running in Japan where Mara spent much of her time. The marathon is so hugely followed there and it is interesting to read about the high-work ethic of the Japanese runners, which definitely reminds me of Mara herself.

Watching Mara running a marathon at her best is very inspiring. She makes it look easy but behind her fantastic running performances are dedication, gruelling workouts and meticulous attention to detail. Mara reminds us that although we continually see advances in watches, apps and other technologies, there is no substitute for hard work and consistent training. She advises runners to never forget to prioritise the basics of tough workouts combined with diligent recovery strategies, rest, and good nutrition.

This book is an invaluable read for anyone aspiring to run their best marathon, coaching endurance athletes and dealing with life's struggles. Everyone will benefit from the helpful strategies provided. It is unique in the way Mara relates wisdom gained through a successful running career to wisdom for life itself. It is both extremely informative and inspiring and a very flowing, enjoyable read.

–*Jo Pavey MBE*
Five-time Olympian, World, European and Commonwealth medallist
European 10,000m champion at age 40
Author of *This Mum Runs*

Acknowledgements

Marathon running is a solitary, individual sport. When I look back over the decades-long journey I travelled, from a sport-mad 11-year-old, to toeing the start line of the 2008 Beijing Olympics women's marathon, I am struck by the sheer number of people who were on that journey with me. Their support, encouragement, patience, selflessness and kindness were fundamental to that journey. Without their help, I am certain I would not have become a world-class marathon runner. It was a team effort, no doubt. I want to record my heartfelt thanks to all of them.

The marathon is a brutal, absurdly competitive event and it takes decades of hard, consistent training to become world-class clean. My parents gave me a physically active childhood in Kenya and Oxford which laid the foundations for an enduring love of sport. My late father, Norman, was the first person who enticed me into running. The P.E. Department at Oxford High School, Headington Road Runners (HRR), Radley Ladies, and Oxford University Cross Country Club (OUCCC) were my home for hours of sport and running training during my younger years. After specialising in endurance running, I benefitted enormously from the expertise of coaches: Julian Goater, Bob Parker, Alan Storey, Bud Baldaro and Michael Woods. I am grateful to all the athletes, officials, team staff and others who, in one way or another, helped me during my years of training and competing.

The years I spent living in Japan as an elite athlete would not have been possible without speaking the language. I am extremely grateful to all my Japanese teachers in the UK and in Japan, and to the Foreign Office, which selected me for the toughest language training available. My teachers' skills, patience and kindness gave me a window into this rich, historic culture that enabled everything in my life that followed. I was able to broaden and deepen this understanding through the warmth, kindness and unequivocal welcome of the extended Yamauchi family. Living, training and competing in Japan was an immensely valuable experience. My thanks go to all the athletes, coaches, officials, team staff and others involved in the Japanese distance running world, whose paths crossed with mine. I am especially thankful to Akemi Masuda, a women's marathon pioneer and wonderful role model.

Distance running can be very tough. But one of its delights is putting yourself through the pain of training with your friends and teammates. No medicine soothes the agony of lung-busting intervals like your comrades suffering with you. My training buddies over the years have become my best friends and I am deeply indebted to all of them. There are so many to thank but to name a few, they include: Megan Clark; Hsu Min Chung; Emma Coleman-Jones and the rest of the OUCCC gang; Andrea Whitcombe; Sally-Ann Cox and all the Parkside stalwarts; Glenys Karran; Namban Rengo; Kamakura FRC and Second Wind AC in Japan; Esther Evans; Ian Higgins; the late Robin Dickson and all the Kingsmeadow group; Susie Bush; Jo Ronaldson and Lucy MacAlister; and my second claim club, Thames Hare & Hounds. When the pain of training is great enough, sometimes you lose your ability to be polite and behave nicely. This makes friendships between training buddies honest, bare and long-lasting. I apologise whole-heartedly to my training partners for the times when, in some shape or form, I have totally lost it out there.

There is no doubt that I would never have run in the Olympics without Shige's help. He accompanied me during training for years; was my coach, agent and manager; completed domestic chores so I did not have to; organised and travelled to training camps and races; massaged my tired legs; negotiated sponsorship contracts; gave up two jobs to help me; and made me see myself as a world-class athlete. Without his support, I would not have been able to train at the level required to compete as an elite athlete. Shige's selflessness, capacity for hard work, curiosity to learn new information, and insightful analysis are unmatched. I was very fortunate to have received his support and am deeply grateful.

Jacques Valentin, a friend from ASICS, came up with the idea of using 42.195 as a structure for this book. A few years ago, I was approached by a Japanese publisher to write a book consisting of a list of my tips and advice to other runners. I began writing such a list off the top of my head, intending later to flesh it out into a full draft. Sitting down and starting to write was like opening the floodgates. I had so many distinct tips in my head. My list quickly became long. After a while, I had jotted down most of them, so I stopped to take stock. I was surprised to find that I had nearly 50 on my list. I set about consolidating them and whittled down my list to about 45 items. Soon after, I had a conversation with Jacques, which resulted in me using the number 42.195. His suggestion reminded me that early in my career I had switched from working in miles to kilometres, reluctantly initially, until I realised how quickly kilometres skip by when you are running ... then I eagerly embraced working in metric. Thank you, Jacques!

I worked for the UK's Foreign Office for many years, in London and Tokyo. I am grateful for its support and flexibility as an employer while I combined work and training. But most of all I am thankful to have worked with so many decent, honest, clever, hard-working and public-spirited people.

Many organisations supported me as an elite athlete. This was my full-time job, and their backing enabled me to pursue running as a professional career. I am extremely grateful to ASICS, my kit sponsor throughout my career. In addition, the following sponsors and supporters provided invaluable support for which I am eternally grateful: Virgin Atlantic; B&D Sports; Yamamoto Kogaku; Meiji Nyugyo; Taiyo Kagaku; Kez Trainer Massage Clinic; PowerBar; The Oahu Club; The Lensbury Club; UK Athletics; UK Sport; Team GB; and the English Institute of Sport.

I am very grateful to my partner, John Herries, for his kindness, patience, humour, unconditional acceptance of me, and unwavering belief in the wonders of strength and conditioning for making the human body function as it should.

This book was in gestation for many years before finally appearing in print. My thanks to everyone who has helped me to turn it into a real book, including my literary agent Wendy Yorke, my editor Anna Yorke and my publisher Meyer & Meyer Sport, especially Liz Evans and Sarah Pursey. I am grateful to all my friends and family who read it in draft, commented, offered ideas, and ultimately played a key role in producing the book you are holding now.

There is not space to mention everyone who has been part of my running life so far, but I am wholeheartedly grateful to every one of them. The responsibility for any errors or omissions in this book lies solely with me.

Introduction:
Always Warm Up!

My journey to becoming an Olympic athlete was unique. I loved all kinds of sports as a child, but was never a serious junior athlete. After leaving full-time education at the age of 22, I worked as a diplomat for ten years. I was 35 years old when I ran in the Olympics for the first time. I am British, but spent my childhood in Nairobi, Kenya, and later I lived in Tokyo, Japan, for most of my career as a full-time athlete. This path was completely unlike that trodden by most elite athletes who typically enjoy their best years at a much younger age and often straight out of education.

This book is a collection of the insights I learned along this unusual journey. I have illustrated them with anecdotes, memories and examples from my running career. Becoming, and then living the life of an elite athlete puts you through a myriad of experiences. From figuring out what you want to do and motivating yourself and others; to making the best of a bad situation and securing enough rest; there is a to-do list that is as forbidding as it is long. Many of these experiences are exhilarating and exciting; others are gut-wrenching and despair-inducing. However, I can safely say that, on this journey of ups and downs, I learned an unimaginable amount – about running, about my character, and about life itself.

I have distilled this knowledge and experience into 42.195 insights in total – the number of kilometres in a marathon. As in a marathon, my book will take you through good times and bad as I explain the thinking, planning and executing that went into transforming myself from an average runner into a world-class athlete. I also explore the nuts and bolts of the marathon: training, fuel, racing, recovery, injuries, goals, and much more. Like the marathon, you might find that the first half cheerfully skips by, but the second half delves into much tougher territory. This is where a lot of learning happens, so please stick with it – even if you hit the wall – right to the end! The conclusion of my book explores that wonderful, magical place – the final 195 metres from the 42km point to the finish line. Each of my insights is self-standing. You can dip in and out of this book, or read it from cover to cover.

This book is for runners of all abilities. Running is a universal sport – it is the same for everyone – regardless of age, ability or background. We all have to get out there and train, cope with injuries, pick ourselves up after disappointing performances and enjoy the thrills of becoming faster. It is solely the speed at which we run which separates us from one another. Unlike in some sports, in the marathon the world's best line up with recreational runners in the same races. We really are all in it together. Although I was an elite athlete, this was only one stage of my running journey. I have also been an average child runner, an obsessed student, and a competitive club athlete. Now since retiring, I am a recreational level masters runner. I have drawn on all these experiences to make this book relevant for runners at all levels. I trust that my insights will resonate and be relatable, whatever level of runner you are.

In addition, this book is also for non-runners because my insights are applicable way beyond running – to life, the workplace, when planning a major challenge – and to athletes in other sports. I hope especially that many female readers will pick up this book and use it. From my observations, women are much more likely than men to lack confidence, hesitate about pursuing their goals, and be vulnerable to persuasion by other people into courses of action which are not in their interests. It would be wonderful if by reading this book, more women and girls felt motivated and equipped to wholeheartedly pursue what they want to achieve.

My desire in writing this book is to help you with whatever goal you are aspiring to. Moreover, I encourage you to use your brain and to acquire or refine the thinking skills which will enable you to create your own programme and goals. Running these days is mass-market business with instructions on how to train, which products to buy, and information overload everywhere. But I hope with this book, you will be able to get away from all that – to step back, see and figure out for yourself what is best for you – and become a better runner. Since I retired from elite competition in 2013, I have done much reflection and learning, and if this book helps you to do the same, I will be delighted! With respect, anyone who was hoping this book would spoon feed them with a standard training manual should stop reading now!

A gentle, brief word of warning: my approach to being good at the marathon, and indeed anything, is a carefully thought-through plan, dedication and hard work. I don't believe in shortcuts or silver bullets. The only way you will become a better runner is specific, consistent hard training, supported by good nutrition, self-care and rest. You will find plenty of useful, practical insights in this book, but no gimmicks – there aren't any! I trust it will help you to perform well in running and other areas of your life.

Right, that is the warm-up completed. It is time to toe the start line. The famous marathon distance brings formidable challenges, self-knowledge and new discoveries to all runners. Are you ready? Let's go!

Part One
Define What You Want to Do

Insight 1
What Fires You Up?

When I was a small child growing up in Nairobi, Kenya, I loved playing outdoors. I ran up and down the steep driveway to our house and dived into all kinds of adventures in the garden. The year-round tropical, warm climate lent itself to spending time outside. I grew up loving sports and being physically active. At weekends and during the holidays, my parents took my sister and me on safari, or to the coast and the Indian Ocean, or any number of exciting adventures under Africa's sun and big skies.

Fast-forward to 1984 and my family had moved to Oxford, England. During that summer, at age 11, I remember watching the Los Angeles Olympics on television and being utterly mesmerised by the sports extravaganza taking place on the other side of the world. The enormous stadium, the glitz and glamour, the athletes giving it their all ... I was transfixed by this spectacle and spent many hours watching it all on television. Strangely, in hindsight I was not really interested in the women's marathon, which was making its hard-won debut in the Olympic Games. Instead, I was focused on the best all-rounders there are, the decathletes and my hero, Daley Thompson. To be able to compete brilliantly in all those various events inspired awe in me, and encompassed what I wanted to be: an all-round athlete. The excitement of watching wore me out and I could not stay awake for the final event, the 1,500m. My mother woke me up in the middle of the night to tell me that Daley had won the gold. After the Games were finished, I watched the BBC's highlights on videotape, set to Spandau Ballet's *Gold*, again and again. After watching those Games, I decided I wanted to be a top-class, world-beating athlete. At age 11, I had no idea how I was going to do it, but from that summer on I had discovered something that really fired me up – a dream of becoming a sporting champion.

Becoming beside yourself with excitement is one of the wonders of childhood. Many children want to be like the fabulous and attractive people they encounter. But if I can describe in general terms what that summer gave me, it was an enduring, aspirational desire to do something special and specific with my life. This desire never left me and always gave me a clear goal to aim and strive for. Between that summer and 17 August 2008, when I finally stood on the start line of my first Olympic marathon in Beijing, 24 years had passed. A quarter of a century! You could say it was not a very motivating or compelling dream since it took me so long to make it happen. But it was not a straightforward journey. I had become side-tracked with other activities along the way, such as earning a living. I believe it is testament to how strong that desire was that it sustained me for so many years to keep going and ensured that I never gave up on my dream.

What I learnt from this burning desire born all those years ago was that discovering a love for something is immensely valuable and worth spending time on. That having a dream which really inspires you provides the engine for hard work, a motivating goal to focus on, and the ability to keep going through hard times. That a love for a particular activity might hit you at a time when you can't do much about it and you might need to return to it later. And that being clear about what you are aiming for is important because it gives you direction and motivation.

Why did it take me so long to realise my childhood dream? Most world-class athletes become professionals straight after or during their full-time education and retire while they are young adults. For me, it was different. When I left university, I wanted to become a full-time athlete but was nowhere near fast enough to earn a living from it. My parents encouraged me to look for a 'proper job'. Like many students, I had no money. Therefore, on leaving full-time education I had no choice and simply had to find a job. I applied to the British Civil Service's Fast Stream graduate recruitment programme and became a diplomat with the Foreign Office. This too was a fascinating adventure. I travelled to places I had never been, had the opportunity to learn Japanese and the privilege of working with issues that mattered. I was posted to the British Embassy in Tokyo and enjoyed further adventures there ... but during all that time, the dream of becoming a world-class athlete was always there in the back of my mind.

When my Tokyo posting came to an end and I returned to London at the age of 29, I decided that if I was to realise my childhood dream, it was now or never.

I spent the next three years working and training hard and finally became a full-time athlete in 2006 at the age of 33. I was 35 when I finished sixth in the 2008 Beijing Olympics women's marathon, the joint best performance ever by a British woman in the Olympic marathon. I was 35 when I set my personal best of 2:23:12 in the 2009 London Marathon. It was a long journey of ups and downs, going off on tangents, and spells when realising my dream seemed like a very distant prospect. But throughout that quarter century, I was always clear what my goal was and what I wanted to be.

Sport is not everyone's cup of tea. Nor is spending a large part of your life pursuing one clear goal. I am not claiming that this is the only way to live a life. But this was my experience. My wish is that by sharing it, you will see how you can pursue and achieve an ambitious goal. We all have talents and gifts of one kind or another, whether it's in sport, music or something else.

> **Having a dream or overall goal provides motivation, direction, and meaning. It might take time, but pursuing what you love is an enriching, life-changing journey.**

Insight 2
From Dream to Reality

My first serious attempt to become a world-class athlete and qualify for the Olympics did not go to plan. In December 2002, I returned to London after my four-year posting at the British Embassy in Tokyo came to an end. I was 29 years old, and newly married to Shige. There were many unknowns waiting for us in our forthcoming new life in London. But time was running out if I was to realise my dream of racing in global championships. Up to that point, I had enjoyed some success in distance running, thanks mainly to my then coach, the late Bob Parker, and his late wife Sylvia, and their formidable group at Parkside (Harrow) Athletic Club, later known as Harrow Athletic Club. They had a thriving group training from their home in North Harrow. Their living room wallpaper famously had a silhouette shaped like the winner's shield from the women's team competition at the English National Cross Country Championships because the shield had hung there for so many consecutive years. But I had only run once for Great Britain (GB) and what I really wanted to do was compete in global championships and become a full-time elite athlete.

In 2003 I was set on making the GB team for the 2004 Athens Olympics. I knew endurance running was my strength but of the three distance events on the Olympic programme at the time, I was doubtful that I could qualify in the 5,000m and 10,000m. I had never had fast natural speed and the qualifying times simply felt out of reach. That left the marathon. So I decided, through a process of elimination, to take on the marathon. Through 2003 I tailored my training to running 2:37, which was the qualifying standard set. I had never run a marathon before and aimed to qualify at the Berlin Marathon in 2003. But *plantar fasciitis* struck in early September and I had to withdraw. Until December 2003 I was resting and rehabilitating my foot. It was January 2004 before I could resume training properly. At the London Marathon in 2004, the trial race for the Athens team, I finished seventh out of the British athletes in 2:39:16 in a debut that included stomach upsets, a stitch, and generally feeling out of sorts. I failed to qualify and make the team.

However, despite the disappointment of not qualifying, on crossing the finish line I knew I could perform much better. In the following year, I paid more attention to my diet, sleep, injury prevention, self-care, mental preparation, and the content of my training. The thanks and credit for all of this go entirely to Shige. He could see where I was falling short, and came up with actual improvements I needed to make in various areas to raise my game. He learned from scratch what the world-beating Japanese female marathon runners were doing to perform at such a high level. All this paid off, and at London in 2005 I qualified for the Helsinki World Championships marathon team by eight seconds (2:31:52). This was a much better performance than a year earlier, and it felt like I was finally on the right track.

The year between these two marathons was the start of an upward trajectory in my performance. The work we put in was not particularly organised, but it worked. I was improving, and we were inching closer towards my goal of racing in the Olympics.

Between having a dream to achieve something special, and actually doing it, there is a huge gulf. What do you actually have to do to make it a reality? What exactly do you aim for, and when? Do you have the money to afford to do it? What support, knowledge and other inputs are necessary? What physical and mental attributes do you need, and do you have them? There are so many questions to answer, it's difficult to know where to start. But you must start somewhere. Whatever your goal is, everyone has to start somewhere. Even champions and world record breakers start out at the bottom and find a way, over time, to reach the top.

For me, the answer to navigating a way to bridge this gulf was creating what I called a roadmap. This was a list of actions and milestones over time, which brought me from merely having a dream to actually competing and performing as an elite athlete at world level. It included: running in particular races on specific dates; the training that was required; the lifestyle changes I had to make to support my training; and the money needed to fund it all. I had already been doing some of this, but in an ad hoc way. Drawing up a roadmap was a helpful way to organise my efforts in a logical and coherent manner. But perhaps the most valuable aspect of this process was not simply the actual content of the roadmap – what I had to do by when – but the fact that it enabled me to see that realising my dream was possible. My roadmap turned a previously vague idea into a realistic, finite sequence of events. In other words, I could see how to actually achieve my goal. This lifted my motivation considerably because I could work hard in the belief that my efforts would actually lead to where I wanted to go.

Having made it to the Helsinki World Championships in 2005, the Beijing Olympics seemed suddenly a realistic goal to aim for. The roadmap I drew up then was clear, focused and realistic. I looked back at marathon qualification standards for GB teams, and at the results of the women's marathons at previous Olympics. To be sure of making the team, and even being competitive in the Olympics, required a time of 2:26 by early 2008. To progress from 2:31:52 in April 2005 to 2:26 by 2008, I decided to aim for increments of two minutes per year, which was realistic and easy enough to aim for. The improvement I had made from 2004 to 2005 showed that my training regime, and all the areas that supported it, was along the right lines, so I continued with it. One valuable lesson I learned during my years of running was this: if you are improving and things are going well, keep doing more of the same. In my impatience to improve more rapidly, later in my career I changed too much and ended up overtraining or injured. I should have stuck more with the routine that was clearly working. If something is not broken, don't waste time and effort fixing it.

Armed with my roadmap to Beijing 2008, I felt confident going into subsequent races with a realistic goal. But as it turned out, I progressed more rapidly than my roadmap, running 2:27:38 in Tokyo in November 2005 and 2:25:13 in London in April 2006. Little more than two years before the Beijing Olympics, having run 2:25 was a fabulous place to be and it gave me so much confidence. I ran 2:25 again at London in 2007 which meant my place on the GB team for Beijing was secure, barring any disasters.

Having a roadmap in your pocket is an invaluable enabler of progress. By defining specific steps and helping you to see the way ahead, it makes realising your dream possible.

Part Two
Achieve Your Dream

Insight 3
Basics, Basics, Basics

In April 2009, I had finished second in the London Marathon with a personal best of 2:23:12 and was ranked second in the world in women's road running. Everything was going well and I was looking forward to that summer's World Championships in Berlin, where I could realistically aim for a medal. But in May, after a short rest and returning to training, I developed *plantar fasciitis* because of a basic and inexcusable mistake. In the excitement and rush of going away on holiday after the London Marathon, I did not pack my trainers, only my racing shoes. While on holiday in Germany, having completed a recce of the World Championships course, I was eager to return to training. I was too impatient and resumed training in my racing shoes rather than waiting until I flew home to Tokyo and could wear trainers. At the time it did not seem like a major mistake. I was used to wearing racing shoes frequently in training and racing, including in marathon races. But I had residual stiffness from the London Marathon, especially in my hamstrings and running in racing shoes gave rise to foot pain that developed into *plantar fasciitis*. In the end, this was the start of several years of persistent and frequent injuries, overtraining, poor performances, excessive fatigue, mental ill-health and eventual retirement. I failed to get right the most basic task for any runner – choosing the correct footwear – and paid a heavy price.

The basics for runners are incredibly simple ... dare I say, even boring! You need to train effectively, fuel and rest well, and ensure you look after yourself properly. The simplest of sports can be enjoyed, to a high level, with a few key ingredients. Performing the basics well seems obvious.

The approach I find most helpful to ensure you get the basics right is as follows. Ignore, for a moment, all external information and focus entirely on yourself. By asking yourself the fundamental questions, you can quickly build up a running routine which will fully address the basics.

» How many times per week can I realistically run?
» Am I completing my routine consistently week after week, and if not, why not?

» What types of runs should I do: easy, steady, intervals, long runs, hills, etc.?
» Am I building up training gradually?
» Is my sleep good enough that I feel rested when I wake up?
» Am I eating a wide variety of foods?
» Is my performance improving, stable or worsening?

These questions may seem all encompassing, but you will notice that they do not include anything about beetroot juice or global positioning system (GPS) watches. That is because they aim to make you think about the fundamentals of your running routine and whether or not they are sound. When I think back to training with my first club, Headington Road Runners in Oxford, it was simple, but the essential elements were there: speed sessions, a long run and steady runs. Nothing flashy, simply doing the basics properly. I remember vividly running the ultimate bread-and-butter speed session for distance runners – mile repetitions – on the Marston Ferry Road cycle track with Headington. Later, I did exactly the same mile repetitions session with Bob Parker's Parkside group. A few key basics are timeless!

However, because we are surrounded by information which is readily accessible, it is easy to overlook how incredibly important it is to do the basics properly. We often see what others are doing and think we must do the same to make progress. Websites, magazines, podcasts, events, social media, coaches, advertising, medical practitioners ... the sources of information about everything running-related are now so numerous and varied that it becomes difficult to judge what is or is not sensible and worth following. Some of the information available may be misleading, conflicting or simply untrue. Elements of it may only make sense in the context of everything else you are doing. Never forget that many sources of advice and instructions may have a primary goal, which is not the same as helping you or your running. For example: a company wanting to sell you more products; a magazine wanting to increase its circulation; a coach wanting to raise their profile and build a name for themselves; a practitioner looking for a runner on whom to try out a new treatment; and race organisers wanting you to enter an event. How do you wade through it all and figure out what to do?

The answer to me is to frequently revisit the basics and ask yourself if you are doing them properly, by using the questions above. Forget about what others are telling you to do for a moment and think entirely about your own routine. Ultimately, you are the one who must develop the understanding of what the basics are and how to do them well. Without this, you risk becoming swayed this way and that and being overwhelmed by the deluge of information available.

When I see information from world-class athletes, such as books they have written or interviews, I often eagerly anticipate learning something exceptional or out of the ordinary. Surely these athletes must have habits or training plans which are somehow exceptional and noteworthy to be so good? However, most of the time, I finish reading such material thinking: oh, none of that was special or surprising – this athlete is merely working extraordinarily hard at training and looking after him- or herself. The majority of top athletes – at least the clean ones – reach the top by sheer hard work on the basics.

By April 2010, I had recovered from *plantar fasciitis* and was regaining good form. I won the New York City Half Marathon in March, a thrilling and unexpected bonus on the road back. Overhauling Deena Kastor, former American marathon record-holder, Olympic bronze medallist, London and Chicago Marathon winner and all-round marathon legend, in the final mile was about the most humbling experience of my career. Thankfully, I recovered from the costly mistake I had made. It was certainly a valuable learning experience.

It is worth returning frequently to the basics and asking yourself if you are optimising them or not. Basics may not be exciting, inspiring or exotic, but they matter the most. I really cannot emphasise the key message of this insight enough.

Do the basics properly before you focus on anything else.

Insight 4
Glorious Goals

Since I retired in 2013, I have coached mainly recreational runners. Often, when I meet a new runner for the first time our conversation follows a similar pattern. They will mention a variety of factors: previous results, training, injuries, work stresses and family events. Often the conversation goes round and round. When this happens, I always stop and ask the runner what their primary goal is. Usually there will be a pause and they will say something quite clear and specific. For example, "I want to break four hours at the London Marathon next year." From there, we work backwards, discuss intermediate races, explore how much training they need to do and by when. Relatively quickly, we arrive at a simple but clear structure for the next few months. Often, the runner will already have thought of all this themselves, but they aren't quite sure if it is the right approach.

What these runners do in these conversations with me is create a set of goals for themselves. This is exactly what I used to do as an elite athlete. The content may be different, but the process is the same. As I said in the Introduction, we runners are all in this together!

Creating meaningful, challenging and inspiring goals is a popular and widely used tool. People in all walks of life, when taking on a challenge, talk about their goals and what lies behind them. If you are aiming to achieve something ambitious, goal-setting is a logical and natural way to organise your efforts. But why do goals provide meaning and structure? It varies from one person to the next.

I always wrote goals for myself and found they were helpful in four principle ways.

1. They made me realise that by pursuing an ambitious goal step by step, I could eventually achieve it. They made apparently unrealistic goals appear possible.
2. They provided a way of organising my daily activities, while ensuring that I spent my time and energy productively.

3. They facilitated the inclusion in my routine of activities which are important but are often overlooked, especially rest and leisure time.
4. When dealing with an injury or setback, they helped me to organise my everyday life in a positive way.

My goals consisted of long- and short-term goals. Long-term goals projected one or more years into the future. I used these goals for deciding which major competitions to target, qualifying for championships, and planning gradual progression towards significant improvements. My long-term goals were similar to the roadmaps I described in Insight 2. But they included more options – in other words, more dreaming!

Short-term goals projected three to six months ahead. The process I used for short-term goals came as a suggestion from the wonderful sports psychologist, Sarah Cecil from the English Institute of Sport. Sarah was always a friendly, reliable and helpful source of sound advice, practical tips and general common sense, which helped me get through numerous difficult times.

My short-term goals sheets might feature a three-month build-up to a major marathon. They included sections about: physical training, mental training, technical aspects, lifestyle activities, rest and time off.

The physical training section complemented and linked to a separate training programme I drew up. But it included my most significant training milestones, such as a longest long run, a time trial, or consistency in training. This allowed me to have an overview of my training over a period of time and to link it to the content of the other sections in my goals sheet. For example, I often used a key long run to test my racing shoes, rehearse my race-day drinks plan, or refine my intended race pace. The physical training section also enabled me to effectively balance my strength and conditioning programme with my running plan.

The mental training section included: practising coping with stressful or anxiety-inducing situations; focusing on the positives, like listing all the hard work I had completed; and creating and then honing a pre-race routine to optimise my mental preparation. The technical section featured activities such as: testing out drinks for a variety of weather conditions; experimenting with racing shoes; and recceing the course of a forthcoming marathon. Lifestyle activities included my goals related to sleep hygiene, body weight and nutrition. Finally, rest and time off addressed the serious business of ensuring I had enough rest and scheduling how and when I did fun activities away from running. Being a full-time athlete can be a mono-dimensional existence; it isn't always healthy. Escaping completely from running from time to time was indispensable for maintaining my enthusiasm and motivation.

My goals sheets were especially useful for scheduling two particular categories of activities. First, the myriad of small preparatory tasks you have to complete before a marathon. This includes: deciding what kit to wear for all possible weathers; wearing in your race-day shoes; deciding and practising how much to drink and when; what warm-up to do; and deciding on race pace. These small tasks are not difficult, but they are important and numerous, so completing them all at the appropriate time can be overwhelming until you have a good scheduling system. Second, experimenting with and trying out new ingredients for your routine, such as alternative types of training, different food or drinks, and the latest model of shoes. All athletes must continually review, progress and adjust their programme to ensure continuous adaptation. Often that calls for experimenting, but doing so at or near to a major race is not desirable. Therefore, time must be found elsewhere for trying out new elements.

My short-term goals sheet included space for recording and monitoring progress and for adjusting goals when my plans went off track – as they often did! Successfully completing every item of work in a plan is extremely rare. The odd omission is not a big deal, but when major alterations are called for, you have to be able to adjust your plan. I often had to rearrange, reorganise, or cut out items altogether from my goals sheet. Despite this, I nevertheless found it immensely helpful to start a three-month preparation block with a clear, structured and written set of goals.

Throughout my running career, I always needed to believe in my training plan – that the sessions I was running had purpose – and that there was clear logic and objective reason behind my daily routine. Training at full tilt for the marathon year after year is, let's be honest, exceptionally hard work. To put myself through that hard work, I wanted to know that it was worth it; that all the effort would result in improvement. In short, I needed to buy in to my regime and I often questioned coaches on why they were recommending certain types of training. My goals sheet was a useful tool for creating this buy-in in my own thinking. I used the clearly set out information on my goals sheet to interrogate the logic and reason behind my programme. If it did not create buy-in for me, I changed it until it did. This iterative process enabled me to have confidence in my programme and commit to doing it to the best of my ability. I learned this process of creating goals as an elite athlete. But my coaching conversations with recreational runners prove to me that this same process is applicable at any level.

Goals provide immensely valuable structure for organising your efforts. Tailor how you use them to suit you and be flexible about adjusting them as progress demands.

Insight 5
Simple Is Best

I recently met the father of a talented young girl who was on the point of quitting running. He desperately wanted my advice about how to keep her in the sport. I asked what the problem was. He said it was social media. His daughter spent every afternoon after a run or race looking at comments her friends had posted. She had become fearful about being judged and anxious about whether or not she looked good enough in photos.

I was so sad to hear this and thankful that I grew up and learned to love running when social media did not exist. It is such a travesty that this talented youngster might quit a simple and enjoyable sport because of the judgment of other people which, on the face of it, has nothing to do with running. I have photos of me running as a teenager which would have attracted howls of laughter and derision on social media if I were a teenager now. I dread to think what the impact of this might have been on me – probably my elite career would never have happened. I have also coached young adults who have descended into meltdown because their GPS watches show a pace a few seconds per mile slower than their friends or what they had expected. Similarly, when I set short, fast intervals for a group, the question will pop up from someone: "What pace should I run?" The definition of short, fast intervals is running them as fast as you can. If you run at a set pace dictated by your watch, they will not be fast intervals. These are all examples of unnecessary complexity diverting attention away from the essence of running.

Running is a simple sport – perhaps the simplest sport there is. You need only clothes and shoes and off you go. You can run whatever distance or speed you want; you can run almost anywhere. We often hear or read about people describing the simplicity of running in this way. Despite this, we excessively complicate it endlessly. We can't help ourselves, encouraged by the free availability of information, social media and the ever-expanding plethora of kit and gadgets marketed at runners. It is tempting to think that pursuing every angle of your running to the finest degree is better. I disagree. I discovered that complexity is a mixed blessing. Resisting it and keeping matters simple is vital. Using up your brainpower and energy on excessively complicating your running will not make you run faster.

In July 2007, I ran the Sapporo International Half Marathon in Hokkaido, in northern Japan. I had already been selected for the 2007 Osaka World Championships Marathon and this was one of my tune-up races. Japan's reigning Olympic marathon champion from Athens 2004, Mizuki Noguchi, and Kenya's Catherine Ndereba, the 2003 World Champion and 2004 Olympic silver medallist, along with several of Japan's top runners, were on the start list. It was a formidable line-up and I was nervous. I ran through my usual preparations and warm-up. I had been thinking about what time I wanted to run and whether I was in personal best shape. But it was an unusual course, with a long steep downhill in the first 5km which we had to climb on return. It was mid-summer in Japan – in other words, it was hot. This complicated my calculations about what time I could aim for and I was struggling to think clearly.

Suddenly, I felt weighed down by thinking too much. I realised that this was not sound mental preparation as the start time rapidly approached. Therefore, I decided to take off my watch, leave it behind and simply race. The current Olympic gold and silver medallists were in the race, for goodness sake! If I could finish close to one or both of them that would be a terrific result regardless of my finish time.

As we set off, I felt relaxed and confident. For most of the race I gave it everything to hang on to Noguchi. In the early stages we ran together. Later on, she opened up a gap but she was always within sight. I finished second to Noguchi in 68:45, taking a huge chunk (39 seconds) off my personal best in hot conditions. I even ran a road 5km personal best of 15:28 along the way to boot. Ndereba finished eighth. For me that race was a brilliant learning experience. By deliberately forgetting about my watch, my pace and the intermediate splits, I was able to focus completely on racing. Mentally I felt fantastic – clear-headed, up for racing and ready to run fast. By stripping away a whole swathe of complications, I produced a much better performance than I believe I would have done otherwise.

A completely different area of running which benefits from simplicity is strength and conditioning. If you think about all the exercises you could do – the equipment gyms are full of – and the different types of strength and conditioning, such as Pilates and yoga, there is endless scope for complexity. It is difficult to know where to start.

I adopt a simple approach: forget about all that complexity and focus on what matters for runners. First, create a menu which is relevant to running by including exercises which have commonality with the running action. For example, single-leg exercises, dynamic exercises done standing up and anything demanding core and hip stability while your limbs move. Second, target the key muscle groups used in running, such as the glutes, hamstrings, calves and abdominal muscles. Third, decide on an amount of any one exercise which leads to a reasonable level of fatigue in that muscle group; this stimulates adaptation and an increase in muscle strength. By using these three simple rules and deciding how often to do strength and conditioning, you can quickly create a useful routine which will help your running.

> **A simple approach can be immensely valuable. Never add complexity unless the benefits are crystal clear.**

First drinks station

Insight 6
Beetroot Juice or Tailored Training?

When I first switched to the marathon, I thought marathon training simply called for increasing the length of the intervals and long runs that I had previously been running for 10km, half marathon and cross country. Then I discovered that several top Japanese women were running much faster marathon times than me, even though I was faster than they were over the half marathon and in training. I learned that this was because I was making a fundamental mistake in one of the most important inputs – training. The marathon, unlike all of the shorter events, is essentially an aerobic event. This is because of its length, 42.195km, and the body's limited carbohydrate storage capacity. To build a big aerobic engine and increase your fat-burning capacity, training at speeds in the middle of your range is crucial. Yet I had been focusing my training on my fast and slow speeds and neglecting the speeds in between. Once I had understood this, I changed my training to include significantly more in the middle range. The result was major improvements in my marathon performances. By ensuring I was spot on with one of the most important inputs into marathon performance – training – good results quickly followed.

The opposite of this is our tendency to become excessively preoccupied with inputs which will have limited impact on performance. For example, runners often ask me questions, such as, "How much faster will I run if I drink beetroot juice before my race?" or "My GPS watch says my VO_2 max[1] is such-and-such, so what half marathon time can I run?" Questions like this show how easy it is for our focus to be side-tracked by these small inputs, at the cost of focusing on what is genuinely important. Identifying and then concentrating our efforts on aspects which will have a major impact on performance is vital.

---

[1] VO_2 max is a measure of the maximum oxygen uptake during exercise. V stands for volume and O_2 means oxygen. In a VO_2 max test, an athlete performs bursts of exercise of gradually increasing intensity, during which oxygen uptake, heart rate, lactate and perceived exertion are measured.

For me, the important inputs for marathon runners can be boiled down to the following.

1. Training – of the appropriate quality and quantity.
2. Rest – especially sleep[2].
3. Fuel – in the form of food and drink.

That is it. Why? Because improvement over time happens in our bodies by a cyclical process known as supercompensation. This consists of stimulus, from training, followed by adaptation, with fuel during rest. If this cycle functions well, the result is improvement over time. If it functions poorly, through inappropriate training, rest or fuel, the result is stagnant or deteriorating performance, and/or injury. This is a relatively simple concept. Using the analogy of baking a cake, this is the process of baking a decent cake with the right ingredients in the correct amounts. Everything else – beetroot juice, fancy kit of various kinds, and all the other gadgets and kit that manufacturers want us to buy – are the extras, the icing on the cake. That is not to say they are redundant. I was an enthusiastic beetroot juice drinker for years. They have their value and can have an impact on performance, but they will never replace training, rest and fuel. There is no point in spending quantities of time and money perfecting a fabulous icing, if you have not made a good cake first. If you want to make big improvements in your marathon performance, you must work hard at prioritising these three important inputs.

Looking in more detail at training specifically, again I apply the principle to prioritise what is important.

1. **Long runs:** the marathon is a long race, so some training needs to be long. How long depends on your training history, how quickly you recover, how physically robust you are, and whether your strength is endurance or speed. Sometimes long runs should include some quality of various kinds, and the pace described in point 3 below, to maximise the stimulus to adaptation. Slow long runs are of limited use.
2. **Long, sustained efforts:** intervals of about four minutes or longer, tempo runs, time trials and races all fall into this category. What they have in common is a high level of effort which you can sustain over a long period of time, up to one hour or more. They demand tolerance of moderately high but stable levels of lactate.

---

[2] I look at sleep and food in detail in Insights 32 and 33.

3. **Aerobic runs which optimise fat-burning:** what I call a fast jog is a pace at which you are just beyond being able to hold a conversation. It is slower than any kind of speed training, but faster than an easy jog. It is the speed at which lactate just starts to creep up from base level and at which fat-burning is maximised.

These three types of training should be the top priorities for marathon preparation if you are aspiring to run fast, however you define that. Everything else, including very fast anaerobic intervals and easy slow runs, is a lower priority. Again, these have their value but it is a question of prioritisation.

Fuel for marathon training is, naturally, one of the top priority inputs. To run a marathon, you have to run far in training, and if you want to improve, some of your training must be fast. All of this needs plenty of fuel – ideally of good quality, with as much variety as possible. When I was training and racing hard, I aimed to do my absolute best with what I was eating and drinking to enable good recovery and adaptation. None of this was complicated; it was simple and focused on the main food groups. It included: ensuring a regular intake of highly nutritious foods such as leafy vegetables, oily fish (grilled eel, unagi, is my favourite), seafood, seaweeds, fermented foods and colourful vegetables; monitoring my hydration status frequently; a protein and carbohydrate snack or drink within 20 minutes of finishing any hard training; and aiming to eat an exceptionally wide variety of foodstuffs. I did not exclude any food groups.

Throughout my marathon career, I always tried to strike a balance between optimising nutrition and the physiological fact that body weight is a major factor in marathon performance. This is not an easy balance to strike. There were times when I tried so hard to keep my weight down for major competitions that my preparation suffered. At the Tokyo International Women's Marathon in November 2008, I had lost weight too rapidly and consequently lost strength. This race had a long uphill section in the last 10km on which I struggled. It was a hard grind and I felt I had lost the strength to power up it fast.

I am a stickler for detail, so maintaining a laser-like focus on the important inputs without becoming distracted by minutiae is a constant challenge. I have to work hard to lift myself out of the detail and see the bigger picture. I always aimed to leave no stone unturned in my preparations for big races. For example, I always made time for a recce of the course for a major marathon, and I kept lists of various foods to make sure I was eating a wide variety of food sources. Up to a point, this was all time and energy well spent. But in the latter stages of my career, I took this too far. I became overwhelmed and exhausted by the level of effort I was devoting to all these details. I spent months trying out numerous slightly different pairs of socks made by a specialist company and recording how each pair felt. Socks are important for any marathoner, mainly if something goes wrong with them, but I already had a model of socks that worked well for me. I now ask myself why did I not simply stick with them and focus my energy on higher priority inputs. A classic example of becoming distracted!

Master the important inputs first; afterwards think about the extras. By all means, be diligent about the details, but these can never be a substitute for doing the important inputs properly.

Insight 7
Too Long a To-Do List

Early on in my marathon career, I combined working at the Foreign Office in London and training. From 2003 to 2006, I worked in two separate job-shares and worked 70% of the time in another job. I woke up early to train and often trained again in the evening. On top of all the other items you have to fit in to life, I barely had any spare time. But this forced me to prioritise and often to say no. I was able to train, recover and work, and I improved rapidly during this time. I concluded that my regime suited me.

When I became a full-time athlete in January 2006, suddenly I had much more spare time. This was valuable initially because it enabled me to rest more, increase my training and ensure I was optimising recovery. But as time went on and I improved further, I became overwhelmed with too much on my plate. This was partly generated by myself and partly from others. I had more commitments as I improved. For example, as I gained sponsorship contracts, I had to fulfil obligations to them. Of course, having sponsors was very welcome and I fully accepted what I had to do for them. But I also made the mistake of allowing my time to become filled with activities which, although running-related, were not high priorities. I thought I was doing my best by taking on these extras. But my rest and time off were what fell by the wayside as a result. Over time, I started feeling exhausted, having little time to switch off and nearing my limits of what I was physically and mentally able to do.

Elite athletes are often heard making claims, such as, "I did everything I could to be the best I could be." If you love a sport and are driven to do your absolute best at it, it is natural to want to do everything you possibly can to maximise your potential. This seems obvious – to reach a lofty goal, you have to work hard, put in the hours, and devote yourself to the task.

However, there is a limit to how far you can take this. We do not have unlimited resources of time and energy each day. Eventually diminishing returns, fatigue and perhaps staleness will creep in. Recognising this early, and adjusting how you are spending your time and energy, is vital.

This point is particularly important for athletes because rest is so critical to performance and recovery from training. If you pack too much into your to-do list, resting will probably be the first activity to disappear. For non-runners, skimping on rest time may not detract from your performance. Indeed, it may be the only way to complete all the work you have to do. But runners simply cannot do this. As soon as you fail to secure enough rest and sleep, training and performance will suffer. While I was an elite athlete, I often had to explain, defend and justify my need for rest to non-runners.

Running, and especially racing, are challenging not only physically, but also mentally. To push yourself through pain requires a huge psychological effort. Runners often describe the mental side of their sport and how they prepare for and cope with its challenges. The importance of rest applies both to our physical and mental capacities. You have to rest both body and mind to perform at your best. If you are physically rested but mentally drained, you will not have the brainpower to push yourself to your limits. Mental rest often calls for turning away from a task and engaging in a completely unrelated activity that is absorbing and fun. This is why I always had a full day off from running once a week or every eight to nine days. I always tried to do an activity on those days which made me completely forget about running and being an athlete. Without this, I became mentally fatigued or stale and started losing the enjoyment of running. The central message I want to emphasise here is that within the finite amount of time and energy we have each day or week, making time for rest and fun away from running is critical; don't simply let all your time become filled up.

The ability to say 'no' is perhaps the most important skill to have, if you are to ensure you use your limited, finite time and energy well each day. I have always found it difficult to say 'no'. I want to please and make life go smoothly. I do not enjoy letting people down. But the cost to yourself and to others can be great if you are unable to say 'no'. Because I found this difficult, I adopted a strategy of trying to educate people in my life about my needs and routine as an elite athlete, including: my need for rest after training or racing; nutritious food I had to eat; the imperative of avoiding infections; having to miss certain events; and treating training like a job which I had to do, no matter what. If your friends, family and colleagues have a good understanding of your life as an athlete, it will be easier for them to accept a 'no' from you when it is called for. After major races, I always tried to schedule a few easier weeks during which I could do more of what I often had to miss when training hard – seeing friends, going out, attending events and travelling.

A typical day when I was training hard for the marathon was full from start to finish, as follows: wake up, eat breakfast, work related to managing my running (for example, races, travel, sponsors, anti-doping whereabouts etc.), train, ice bath and shower, lunch, sleep, massage/physio, second training session, shower, dinner, more work, go to bed. I went straight from one activity to the next and the whole day would pass by with training, rest, fuelling and other essential tasks. I had little spare time or energy for anything else. I have often been asked what I did all day, but believe me, training for the marathon at elite level can easily become a full-time job. Eventually, if I was considering or asked to add more into my routine, I had to identify what I could drop from it to make space for something new. I have concluded that this is a good strategy for ensuring you are using your time and energy efficiently. It is easy to fall into the trap of always wanting to do more, believing that this will help you to improve. But we all have limited resources. In summary, my advice to runners and non-runners alike is as follows.

> **Accept that your time and energy are finite. Resist adding ever more to your to-do list. Be ready to say 'no'. Ensure you have enough rest to maintain your enthusiasm.**

Insight 8
The Art of Copying

Clyde Hart, coach to sprint legend Michael Johnson, once reportedly said, "You don't get to be a good coach without being a good thief" and "It is important to learn or 'borrow' ideas from others." Hart was talking about what I call the art of copying – using what you see others doing, but adapting, altering and honing it for your own uses. This is an invaluable tool for all runners, but you have to use it carefully. I copied from other people throughout my running career. But I learned that to be truly useful, copying must be accompanied by good self-awareness and sound judgement.

The word 'copy' has a slight negative connotation to it – simply using others' ideas and skills while lacking any creativity or initiative of your own. But, in the real world, copying underpins everything we do: children learn by copying their parents; scientific progress relies and builds on the discoveries of the past; and creative artists draw inspiration from what they see and experience around them. The art of being a successful copier, for me, is in shaping what others are doing for your own uses, by applying your own knowledge, understanding and creativity. Of course, you must also give credit where it is due.

Copying is everywhere in distance running. We want to know how world-beating athletes train so we can emulate them. Youngsters become inspired by top stars and want to be like them when they grow up. Coaches seek to use successful methodologies from the past with new generations of athletes. Running is an ancient activity which humans have been pursuing for a very long time. There are fundamental facts about running physiology which never change, although our understanding of them might become more refined over time. Therefore, avoid wasting time and energy reinventing the wheel. It is more productive to spend your energy on applying already well-known facts to yourself as an individual – in other words, learning the art of copying.

I learned from and copied Japanese athletes in numerous ways, because I lived in Japan for most of my elite career. Japan is, without doubt, a superpower in women's marathon running.

The first item I copied was their race day breakfast menus. Before my first marathon, London 2004, I ate cereal for breakfast. It was a source of carbohydrates and was my regular breakfast menu, so I thought eating what I was used to was a good start. However, I had to pay several visits to the toilet during the race and had a disappointing run. I concluded that my race-day breakfast needed to change. Shige studied what Japanese athletes ate for their race-day breakfasts. One answer was *mochi* rice cakes, *miso* soup, a boiled egg, small amounts of vegetables and orange juice. This menu provided carbohydrate, salt, fluid, protein to reduce the glycaemic index of the mochi, and a little fibre. I decided it was a good menu, so I practised it in training, and ate it before my next marathon, London 2005. That race was an enormous improvement on the previous year; I knocked more than seven minutes off my personal best, and earned selection for the Helsinki World Championships. I can't say that my new breakfast menu was the only cause of my improvement, but it certainly helped. From then on, I ate the same breakfast before every marathon with confidence that it suited me and contained a suitable mix of macronutrients.

Training methods were another element of the formidable women's marathon scene in Japan that I copied. From observing Japanese athletes doing slower training than me, and yet running faster marathons, I understood that I needed to include more aerobic, and less anaerobic training in my routine, as described earlier. However, there were numerous other aspects of Japanese training which I tried copying, but then abandoned because they did not suit me. Several of Japan's marathon legends, including 2000 Sydney Olympic champion Naoko Takahashi, 2004 Athens Olympic champion, Mizuki Noguchi, and 2004 Berlin Marathon champion, Yoko Shibui, were famous for running enormous quantities of kilometres per week. I heard that Shibui sometimes ran 20km in the morning as her easy run before the 'real' training for the day even began. A large volume of training per week is considered essential for marathon success. Therefore, I believed I had to do the same to be successful. But running large volumes invariably left me exhausted, overtrained, or injured. No doubt my advanced age as an elite athlete accounted for some of this. Eventually I learned that while this approach may work for some runners, it simply did not for me. I had to stop trying to do the impossible. A critical part of mastering the art of copying is to recognise quickly when an idea which works for others does not work for you and to limit the amount of time you spend in denial about this.

An invaluable attribute for learning the art of copying is having an objective and realistic understanding of yourself as an individual. This will provide a solid foundation against which to judge all the information you come across. It enables you to decide what to try copying and what to ignore. For me this was and still is, a work in progress.

Since I started coaching, I have concluded from observation that many runners have benefitted from developing their knowledge of themselves. I often see runners who have copied what they have seen or heard from their teammates, magazines, websites and elsewhere and had a bad experience from it. This includes, for example, choices of footwear, types of training, eating habits and strength exercises. They feel they must copy everything that is reportedly good out there, because it comes from reputable sources or faster runners. They end up confused and frustrated as to why their efforts have not worked out. I am certainly guilty of this myself. For years, I sought out what the best were doing, copied anything and everything under the sun, and tried to add more and more to my routine. But at the same time, I failed to carefully consider my age, my training history, my goals, and the injuries I was prone to. Furthermore, I took this approach in spite of the fact that for several years I had been improving and performing well. How I wish now that I had been more judicious in assessing what was worth copying and ignoring the rest.

The night before the 2005 Tokyo International Women's Marathon, Shige and I went to have dinner at an *udon* restaurant in Tokyo's Akasaka-Mitsuke district near the race hotel. *Udon* are carbohydrate-rich noodles. I had unashamedly copied Naoko Takahashi in this, after reading that she ate *udon* the night before a big race, with a few *mochi* rice cakes thrown in for good measure. We took our own *mochi* and asked the waiter if the chef would microwave them and add them to my *udon*, which he kindly agreed to do. While we waited for our food, to our surprise, Takahashi and her entourage arrived and sat in the room next door to us, separated only by paper walls. I knew she was in the race too, but to be almost rubbing shoulders with marathon royalty in the same restaurant was beyond exciting! Race day arrived, and Takahashi made a stunning comeback to top form, after failing to make Japan's 2004 Olympic team the previous year, while she was the reigning Olympic champion. Meanwhile I finished fifth, having been up there with the leading group in the first half, and setting a personal best by about four minutes. I was thrilled with my performance, and we made a point of returning to the *udon* restaurant the following day to thank the staff. The chef was a bit nonplussed by my fifth place, casually remarking, "You only had four *mochi* in your *udon*; Takahashi had *five!*"

Copying may be frowned upon by some people. But life is short and reinventing the wheel takes time. After seeing mixed results from attempting to copy others, I concluded that there is more to it than meets the eye. I agree with Clyde Hart, but if I were to adapt his message to make my own version (see what I did there?), the following is what it would be.

Copy others, but always with good self-knowledge and objective judgement. Have the courage to ignore others' ideas when they do not suit you.

Insight 9
Open Your Mind

At the London Marathon in 2009, the start list included the three 2008 Olympic medallists, two of whom were also 2007 World Championship medallists; the 2008 Berlin Marathon champion; and numerous others with personal bests that were faster than mine. From looking at the start list, a top-ten finish would have been respectable for me. I tried to ignore all the awe-inspiring biographies of my rivals, focus entirely on my own performance and be open-minded about the time I could run. Admittedly, I was helped by completing a VO_2 max test six days before race day, which indicated I was in 2:21-22 shape. On race day, I tried to be open to the possibility of running better and faster than I ever had before and not to impose any limits on myself. I simply concentrated on producing the best performance I was capable of on that day and I finished second.

We runners tend to be creatures of habit. Familiar routines bring consistency, comfort and simplicity, which can help to make the hard work of training easier. Habits are less arduous for our brains to process than new challenges, so it's easy to see how we can quickly fall into them. Over years of observing habits in myself and other runners, I came to understand how vital it is to have an open mind in order to improve. What I actually mean by this is as follows.

1. Expose yourself to new ideas, novel ways of thinking and operating, and spending time with other athletes.
2. Be willing to try out new approaches, when competition allows.
3. Revisit frequently the logic, reason and evidence behind your routine.
4. Take a fresh look, from time to time, at your habits and interrogate whether they are still fit for purpose.

I have met runners who have adopted habits which they believe are sound. When they decided to start doing a particular activity, they satisfied themselves that it was a good idea based on compelling information. From then on, they did it repeatedly and it became a habit. This can be in any area of running, for example, training, nutrition, warm-ups, resting and competition. However, over time, this habit may no longer be relevant or suitable. Yet because they started it in a positive way, they do not change the habit. Examples I have come across include: going to sleep after an evening training session without eating; running three hard days consecutively; and sticking with strength and conditioning exercises beyond their usefulness.

I have fallen into similarly bad habits myself because I did not follow the crucial elements of having an open mind, described above. Early in my marathon career, I had been focusing entirely on anaerobic speeds and easy running, because this was the menu I knew from training as a younger athlete for cross country, 5km and 10km. I was too wedded to this received wisdom and was unwilling to fully consider other ways of training.

In 2005-6, some interesting results forced me to pay attention and open my mind. At the Helsinki World Championships Marathon in August 2005, Japan's Harumi Hiroyama finished eighth in 2:25:46. A long way behind her, I finished eighteenth in 2:31:26. A few months later, in February 2006, the finishing order was reversed at the Kagawa Marugame International Half Marathon, where I ran 69:24 to her 70:59. I thought I had progressed in the intervening months. In March, she then ran a brilliant 2:23:26 to win the Nagoya International Women's Marathon. Inspired by her victory, and our relative results at Marugame, I lined up at the London Marathon in April feeling sure I could run about 2:22. I ran 2:25:13. This was a personal best, but I could not understand how, having been well ahead of her over the half marathon, I was way behind her in the marathon.

I spent time trying to figure this out, including looking more at how Japanese athletes trained. I concluded that much of my training remained too fast, and too tailored towards the shorter anaerobic events. I had already started to change my focus more towards speeds in the middle range, especially what I call a fast jog. This experience made me realise how overdue that change was, and confirmed that it was the correct approach for the marathon. I regretted not having been open to other ways of training much earlier, and having failed to learn sooner from others. I wished I had listened more, been more receptive to new ideas and questioned the basis of the training I had become used to from my younger days.

The value of an open mind is critical in competition. This is especially true when you are trying to push the boundaries, set personal bests, or perform well above what you might expect. If you are trying to break new ground, by definition, you must have an open mind, to allow what you have never done before to happen. In this context, I believe the concept of marathon race pace should only come into focus in the final few weeks before a marathon. Its purpose then is to help you to decide the pace at which you will set off. Until that point, the focus of any training routine should be improvement. I have seen so many runners set themselves a marathon race pace target early which is way too easy for them. They become wedded to this pace, which means too much of their training is too slow. A rough ballpark target race pace may be useful early on, to give a sense of direction. But keep this loose and be open to adjusting what you think you are capable of right up until race week.

When I first moved to Japan in 1998, I found the urban environment and lack of green space quite disheartening. Yet the Japanese love their running, so I decided there must be lovely running terrain available – it was simply a question of finding it. But the more I looked, the more I discovered that many runners in Tokyo were training on circular, urban loops, including the famous 5km circuit around the Imperial Palace and the 1.3km Gaien loop at Sendagaya. I did not find this inspiring at all. I longed for huge parks and countryside where you never have to retrace your steps – like I was used to running in back home. Reluctantly, I accepted my new running environment and started training on these loops. To my surprise, over time I began to like and even love them. They certainly improved my mental strength. They broke down longer runs into smaller chunks, and training was always simple – only a question of how may laps. I am so glad that the relative lack of green space forced me to open my mind to training on these loops and discover what was positive about them. A few years later I did a 35km run around seven laps of the Imperial Palace – quite mentally tough, I thought, until I heard about the Gaien loop being used by Japanese runners for 40km+ long runs!

Switching to technology for a moment, GPS watches are ubiquitous in distance running now. I have mixed views about them, primarily because they appear to have the effect of closing, rather than opening, runners' minds to what is possible. So many runners now seem to train at a pace dictated by their watches, not by how they feel or the desire to go faster. This problem is compounded by the fact that GPS watches are not always accurate anyway. When I see a runner's mind becoming closed by their GPS watch, I always suggest that they try a training run or even a race without their watch. My instructions to my coachees about racing without a watch are always the same, "Run from start to finish, as fast as you can." Simple! That's what racing is.

A further reason why I encourage – sometimes – running without a watch is this: being able to judge and control your effort is a valuable skill that all runners should learn. Watches are a distraction and don't help with this. One of my former sponsors, B&D Sports, organised a run for their staff while I was living in Tokyo and asked me to join. The distance was 20km, to be run without a watch and we all had to declare our estimated finish time in advance. I decided to run at my fast jog pace, which then was roughly four minutes per km, so I declared 80 minutes. I finished within a few seconds of this! I had never joined a challenge like this before, but realised that by doing hundreds of hours of training at this pace, I had learnt exactly what that effort felt like.

I am so fortunate and grateful that I grew up and fell in love with running before this technology existed. Call me old-fashioned, but the value of an open mind is worth more than your latest mile splits.

> **An open mind is an invaluable asset. Habits and routines make our lives easier, but be ready to change them if necessary. Always make room for new ideas, concepts and possibilities.**

Part Three

Mental Strength and Confidence

Insight 10
Focus on Yourself

While competing as an elite athlete, I always compared myself to the absolute top athletes in the world. This may have driven me on to higher goals, but it also led to a chronic lack of confidence which had a negative effect on my training and performances. I remember, while training in St. Moritz for the 2008 Beijing Olympics, spending hours reading about other athletes on the Internet and feeling a steady draining away of confidence. If only I had realised what was happening and forced myself to stop doing it. Even after the Olympics, I should have been thrilled by coming sixth. But there was a slight nagging disappointment about missing out on the medals, lacking the required change of pace in the closing stages and not quite being good enough. Now that I look back, all of this seems absurd. Sixth place is the best performance ever by a British woman in the Olympic marathon, also achieved by Priscilla Welch in 1984, and my initial goal was only to make the GB team. Compulsively comparing myself with the best in the world had left me feeling that sixth place was somehow inadequate. However good a performance is, there is always more an athlete can achieve. An Olympic or world champion can always win another title, complete a set of titles, or break records. There is no end to possible achievements.

'Compare and despair' is a phrase we often hear. It describes the unhelpful habit of comparing yourself with high achievers and feeling inadequate, left behind, or simply not good enough. Newspapers, magazines, social media, television, the Internet and other sources are full of stories about people achieving incredible, superhuman success. Let's be honest: there is little money in stories about average folk being ordinary, and yet that is what most of us are doing every day. The wall-to-wall coverage of talented people can feel like everybody is achieving fabulous success all the time, but it is only a tiny minority of people.

It is the same in the running world. Winners, champions and record-breakers are all over the media. Even if you are not aspiring to be an elite athlete, it can be depressing at times always reading about runners who are on top form and going places. There is a lot of hard graft in running – dealing with injuries, training in bad weather and coping with fatigue – and we don't often see much coverage of this. Behind every glamorous, awe-inspiring Olympic gold-winning performance are years, perhaps decades, of hard work which we rarely see.

My answer to 'compare and despair' is simply to focus on yourself and do your absolute best every day. Forget about how fast your friends have run, what mileage others claim to have run, or how fit somebody else looks. At the end of the day, you cannot control what others do; you can only change yourself and your own behaviour.

The 2006 Commonwealth Games 10,000m was a race in which focusing on myself served me well. I was well down the field on the start list, but felt I had improved a lot in the weeks and months since I had last raced 10,000m. In the hours before the race, I found a quiet corner of a room in the athletes' warm-up area and sat there by myself. I did not want to have to make conversation with anyone. I wanted to be left alone so I could focus totally on myself – to rest up, visualise the race and do my pre-race routine without interruption or distraction. I decided that the only way I could be near the front in the final laps was to hang on to the leaders for as long as I could. Once big gaps appear in a 10,000m race, it's difficult to close them. It was perhaps a rather passive race plan, simply staying with whoever else was making a go of it, but it worked.

Four of us got away from the rest of the field and that is how most of the race went by. As we neared the end, I became fearful of finishing fourth. Sure enough, I was dropped by the other three athletes with a few laps to go. Again, I tried to focus on myself – to keep going as fast as I could – to remember that others were suffering too and to not allow the race to be over in my own head while it was still going. After a short time in no-man's land, like a miracle, the gap to third-placed Benita Willis of Australia started to visibly close. Suddenly, the possibility of catching her became real and there was enough of the race left to close the gap. I managed to claw my way back and win the bronze medal. For someone who lacks natural speed, winning a medal on the track was strange; I had a huge attack of imposter syndrome. I felt terrible for Benita afterwards, pushing her into fourth in front of a home crowd in the packed Melbourne Cricket Ground stadium. We had trained together in Teddington and at the previous year's World Cross in France. Overall, this race turned out well because at various stages I focused totally on myself and did not allow myself to be distracted by, or lose confidence because of what others were doing.

Running, of course, is not the only activity in which focusing on yourself can be useful. When I was a teenager at school, I had a little ritual for the moments before the start of exams, when the invigilating teacher was handing out the exam papers. I covered my eyes with my hands and said to myself, "Do your best. You can do this."

In that brief moment, I shut out the room and everything in it and set myself up to simply give my best.

The phrase 'focus on yourself' is straightforward, but what does it actually boil down to in concrete terms? Asking yourself the following self-awareness raising questions can make you focus on yourself and understand where there is scope for making progress.

- » What training has worked well for me in the past?
- » How much sleep per night do I need to function well?
- » What activities make me feel energised and cheerful?
- » When I feel down, are there causes which crop up again and again?
- » What do I need to eat regularly to stay healthy?
- » What bad habits do I have which leave me feeling low?
- » What is my plan for the next race or block of training?
- » Am I planning enough fun things and time off?

By answering these questions honestly and in as much detail as you can, you will develop a good understanding of what you need to function well and to be the best you can be. The act of spending time and energy thinking about these questions will stop you from thinking about other people. Displacement activity is often a runner's best friend!

> **Comparing yourself with others is rarely helpful. You and your behaviour are what you can control. Concentrate on that and do your best at it.**

A quarter of the way there!

Insight 11
Process or Outcome?

In April 2004, after I failed to qualify for the Athens Olympics, Shige convinced me to focus on what I was doing away from training, including: nutrition, self-care, recovery, stretching and massage. He thought I was focusing far too much on training and neglecting all the other factors. He was right. I had not thought carefully enough about all these areas which support training. Training was, so I thought, all that really mattered. The truth is, I did not really know what to do to improve on many of the non-training elements anyway. We gave all these areas a thorough audit and overhaul and started to work much harder on all of them. Despite putting more effort into all these factors, it did not feel at all like a burden. Rather, I felt good about myself for doing my level best on them. Soon after, I started to improve rapidly and the benefits of stepping up became abundantly clear.

The term 'process goals' describes what we were doing on all these areas. We were working hard at all the daily processes – eating nutritious food, sleeping enough, massage to prevent injury, etc. – which are not an end in themselves, but contribute to an outcome goal, namely, running faster.

The aforementioned sports psychologist, Sarah Cecil, introduced me to the concept of process and outcome goals. We worked together on this for many years and it became an immensely useful and positive contribution to my running.

Many goals that runners use are outcome goals; for example, running a set time in a marathon, breaking a personal best, or winning an age-group category. They are about completing a clearly defined, concrete task. There is value in this because an outcome goal gives clear direction to your efforts and you can say objectively whether you have achieved it or not – and there is a sense of a finite journey with an end destination. Many people find outcome goals motivating and inspiring. They serve to provide an overall aim on which you can build smaller goals and are something to aspire to.

By contrast, process goals are about conducting your day-to-day activities, or processes, to the very best of your ability. Examples include: training six times per week; eating five fruit and vegetables per day; sleeping for eight hours per night; stretching for ten minutes after every run; and learning three new warm-up drills by a set date. If you are organised and committed, it is relatively straightforward to do them.

Outcome and process goals have their pros and cons. Outcome goals, while providing motivation and something to aim for, can also create fear and anxiety, which will almost certainly detract from performance. There are numerous factors – including the weather, unforeseen events, and accidents – which are out of your control. These factors might prevent even the best-prepared athlete from achieving an outcome goal, despite their training having been optimal. Simply having an outcome goal does nothing, in real terms, to help you reach it – you still have to complete all the hard work to be physically able to achieve it. Outcome goals create pressure which may or may not be helpful. This may be from yourself, but also from other people. I remember the brilliant Charles van Commenée commenting to me soon after the Beijing Olympics that it was possible for me to win the 2012 Olympics Marathon. It was flattering to hear my name and winning a home Olympics being mentioned in the same breath by the UK Athletics head coach, but it also created pressure. Process goals, while being straightforward to do, may seem humdrum and unexciting compared to lofty and ambitious outcome goals.

Both these types of goals are linked. Using them effectively to complement each other can be a great way to progress your running skills. Making outcome goals which are useful, achievable, and realistic, boils down to creating and implementing sound process goals. For example, suppose you are aiming to set a personal best for 10km, but are suffering from excessive fatigue in training. A useful process goal might be having a blood test and, depending on the result, eating more iron-rich foods if your iron is low. This process goal will contribute to achieving your outcome goal by enabling you to train more effectively.

I have had excessive, unwelcome anxiety for most of my life. Outcome goals, I discovered, often felt overwhelming or difficult to reach, especially if others expressed high expectations of me. I often used to dwell too much on an upcoming race, which simply fuelled this anxiety. By contrast, process goals were a blessing as they were often relatively small, undemanding activities – and a helpful way to organise my time and effort constructively. Simply focusing on process goals was incredibly liberating and encouraging. After all, doing your best every day will make it more likely that you will achieve your outcome goals.

I firmly believe that using process goals is by far the best way of coping with periods of injury. You do not know when an injury will end, so it is difficult to set any kind of meaningful outcome goals in terms of running. The outcome goals you previously had may seem remote, or even completely unachievable. Mental health can quickly deteriorate during injury lay-offs because you have lost so much of the enjoyment of running – being out in the fresh air, the routine, and seeing your friends. Motivation can quickly evaporate. But focusing on process goals gives you something useful and constructive to work at and it keeps you occupied when you would otherwise be running. But most of all, process goals will help you to recover from an injury and return to running.

In the first half of 2011, I had a chronic, high hamstring tendinopathy and was not running for nearly six months. I was working hard at a comprehensive rehabilitation programme, but for whatever reason, my hamstring was not recovering. My outcome goal, competing in the London 2012 Olympics, was approaching fast and I had to qualify and earn selection. This gigantic outcome goal loomed ahead of me, increasing the pressure and anxiety every day that I could not run. After resisting having surgery in June 2011, I changed tack and started really focusing on glute activations. With the help of coach Dan Pfaff, I realised that the glutes on my injured leg were not activating well at all, so we set about fixing this to offload the hamstring. To ensure good activation, I performed single-leg glute bridges and explosive step-ups immediately before every run I attempted. Within 48 hours, the pain was starting to subside and I was able to start running in small amounts. As soon as any pain restarted during a run, I stopped, found a step and repeated the explosive step-ups to reactivate my glutes before resuming my run. Sometimes I could run for only fifteen minutes and within that I had to stop five or six times.

Eventually I was able to string longer pieces of running together with fewer stops. From having not run at all between January and June 2011, I recovered my fitness, qualified and secured selection onto Team GB by early December. It was like a miracle, except it wasn't. It was simply and mainly down to using the process goal of performing glute activations diligently every day. By focusing my efforts, I was able to make progress and displace my anxiety about the Olympics. To be frank, by June 2011 I was starting to resent the outcome goal of running in the 2012 Olympics. All it was giving me was pressure and anxiety. But by December 2011, thanks to that process goal, my outcome goal had become realistic and appealing again. I was on Team GB and excited about going to a second Olympics.

Another example of how a training process goal helped my performance was in my preparation for the 2008 Beijing Olympics. We spent the summer of that year training at altitude in St. Moritz. A friend, Adrian Marriott, kindly joined us for some sessions. In one track session we ran together, he suggested I practise my sprint finish from a specific point. My final finishing speed was never that good and I had often been out-sprinted in the closing stages of races. We practised running eyeballs out for the last 150 metres of each interval. The goal was changing pace decisively to drop any rivals and hold the gap until the finish. Fast forward to the Olympics later that summer and I entered the Bird's Nest stadium at the end of the marathon shoulder-to-shoulder with one of the Russian athletes. Knowing I was out of the medals, there was no way I was going to let her beat me. I knew exactly what to do, as practised in St. Moritz. With 150 metres to go, I changed gear decisively, dropped her and finished two seconds ahead of her. This was a process goal that was familiar, well-practised and it served me well.

Outcome goals are a mixed blessing. They provide inspiration but also pressure. Working hard every day at process goals will – in the end – help you to perform at your best.

Insight 12
Your Unique Toolbox

Performing a recce of the course before a major race was one activity which I discovered boosted my confidence immeasurably. Before the second time I ran the London Marathon, in 2005, we trained on sections of the course early on Sunday mornings about five times. I knew the course already and began to think that five times was a bit excessive. But I realised that the act of performing a recce – going there in person, seeing it with my own eyes and feeling what the course was like – had a huge positive impact on my mental outlook. On race day, I knew exactly where the drinks stations, undulations, speed bumps, corners, patches of rough tarmac, and mile markers were coming up. It made the marathon feel like a familiar, simple task which I could tick off easily, not a gruelling long journey which I should fear. I concluded from this that recces were a beneficial and positive tool I could use to get an edge on my rivals. They were something that I discovered worked for me – an easy win. Thereafter, I always made time for a thorough recce of any marathon course, if travel logistics allowed. For the Helsinki, Osaka and Berlin World Championships, the Beijing and London Olympics, and the New York City Marathon, I made special trips ahead of time to see and run on the course. For the London Olympics, like for the London Marathon, I trained on the course numerous times. It was a twisty-turny, multi-lap course with undulations, cobbles and the Guildhall courtyard which, if wet, was like a skating rink! Because I was living in London, I was able to practise on the course which was a huge advantage for me compared to athletes from other countries. I also set up twisty-turny courses in my local park to practise running fast round tight corners.

Improving at distance running boils down to finding out what works for you, and then repeating it over and over, to gain long-term improvement. The obvious area this applies to is training, but there are many others: your pre-race mental routine, nutrition habits, choice of running shoes, injury-prevention measures, sleep hygiene, recovery strategies, and managing work-life balance. Some of these may be common to most runners, but many are quite individual – what suits one person may be completely unlike what suits another. Despite all the arguments for eating carbohydrates before races, I have met a few runners who simply can't run after eating. They skip race-day breakfast altogether and manage with what they can fill up on in the preceding days. It is worth spending time experimenting to find out what works for you.

Having a written record of what works for you is useful, so I always wrote down habits or activities that suited me. This is helpful because the content of what you do suits you, but also because it will give you confidence. If you have a written toolbox of items that work for you, you don't have to spend any mental or physical energy on weighing up options or making decisions. It can even be liberating approaching a big challenge armed with this knowledge. This is why I often found the final few days before a marathon less stressful than the preceding weeks. I had completed all the hard work and what remained was merely executing a well-planned and thought-through process which I knew I was capable of doing. In a strange way I looked forward to race day.

I discovered many small, practical habits which worked for me through experimenting and copying others.

1. I have always had cold feet and hands in winter and been prone to foot injuries. During the winter months, I used to plunge my feet into a bucket of hot water for a few minutes immediately before any quality training. Once my feet were warmed up, I dried them, put my shoes on and went straight to training.
2. For several years, I used aromatherapy oils on my skin as a form of self-care. Many people are sceptical of such treatments, but I found they really helped my recovery. Essential oils have a range of properties that are helpful for runners, including anti-inflammation, encouraging circulation, reducing anxiety, stimulating the nervous system, cooling and warming.
3. My recovery smoothie consisting of soy milk, honey, banana, sesame seeds and recovery drink powder helped to speed up my recovery after hard sessions.
4. My race-day breakfast as described in Insight 8 was a tried-and-tested formula that I knew would work; I never changed it.
5. Early on, I wrote down my race-week routine. This included training, what I would eat and when, any travel to the race, sleeping hours, mental visualisation, packing my race bag, practising catching drinks bottles, doing a recce of the course, deciding my race plan, attending any race meetings, massage, physio, obligations to sponsors, and resting time. This routine worked well but I occasionally adjusted it if something was not quite right.

'If you find something that works for you, stick with it', is perhaps most important when it comes to training. It is worth revisiting the process of supercompensation here to understand why. In summary, training inflicts damage on the body such as muscle micro-tears and fuel-depletion. In response to this stimulus, your body adapts in various ways. You then train again, and the process of adaptation is repeated. This cycle of supercompensation happens over and over, and after a period of time the result will be objective improvement. This is what happens when the cycle of adaptation is working well, and you are becoming faster over time. If your performances are stagnating or worsening, the cycle is not working optimally for some reason. Therefore, if you arrive at the fortunate position of improving over time, you can deduce that your cycle of adaptation is working well. In this case, there is a strong argument to continue your routine exactly as it is. The only scenario that is better than this is improvement at a faster rate. If, after more time, your improvement falters or stops, then that may be the time to change your routine.

I often use this concept when coaching. A runner may tell me they want to break, say, three hours for the marathon. When discussing their training, I always start by explaining the paragraph above. You need to find a training regime which causes you to improve. If that happens, keep doing it. If you are not improving, we need to change the regime. Whether or not that results in a sub-three marathon, I can't predict. But spending as much time as possible on an improving, upward curve will maximise the chances of reaching that goal.

Clearly, age is closely related to our ability to improve. After a certain age, we can no longer expect to run actual personal bests, though plenty of runners in their forties, fifties and beyond do. Therefore, what you define as 'improvement' in the above model needs to be adjusted appropriately for senior runners.

Discovering what works for you is a real blessing. When it happens, take careful note and repeat it in the future. This will save you valuable time and energy and boost your confidence.

Insight 13
Value Your 'Done' List

In the Spring of 2005, I was training for the London Marathon with the aim of qualifying for the World Championships in the marathon. My plan was tailored towards marathon training. I loved cross country and raced it occasionally, but my training was designed for the marathon, not cross country. At the National Inter-counties, I was the first finisher not to be selected for the World Cross Country Championships team. I wasn't disappointed because it was not part of my plan. But at the last minute, due to a withdrawal, I was offered a place on the team as a late addition. Although not training specifically for cross country, I could not miss this opportunity. But I felt underprepared and lacking speed. If there is one event where you really suffer if underprepared, it is cross country. The pain begins right at the start and never stops! On race day, being the last to make the team, I started off at the back of the pen and was last of the GB athletes as we got underway. But gradually I moved through the field past all my teammates and finished 27th. This was a much better result than I had hoped for. Throughout the whole experience, from the trials to being selected to race day, I felt behind the curve and was desperately trying to simply keep up.

This is an example of how not being fully prepared for a competition often leads to a better performance than if you have accomplished a perfect build-up. If you have not quite completed all the preparation you had planned, missed some training, had time off through illness or injury, it leaves you feeling left behind, eager to catch up, and anxious to get even again with your rivals. This feeling is uncomfortable, no doubt. But in my experience, it is an excellent way to start a race. It gives you hunger and a desire to make up for what you have lost. Above all, it means physically you will be better rested than if you had been training at full tilt all along.

Why is this important? Because it illustrates why valuing everything you have done, as opposed to worrying about what you haven't, is so important. If you focus too much on what you have missed – training lost to injuries, spells of illness, or races cancelled – there is a danger that you will compensate or make amends, by doing extra cross-training, or catching your training up in a short period of time. The result is likely to be overtraining. If you are so focused on doing everything in your training plan, come what may to avoid missing a single session, you are more likely to overcook it. The symptoms of overtraining are fatigue, irritability, loss of motivation for training, poor sleep, and lack of enjoyment. Any one of these symptoms make racing tough, but all of them together certainly make for a difficult and unpleasant experience. Very few top athletes go into competition perfectly prepared. Most will incur injuries, illness or other setbacks along the way. At major global championships, we often see elite athletes competing who have missed training, have injuries, or for whatever reason are not fully prepared. But often, the gaps in their preparation do not matter in the end. They have prepared enough to perform well. What they have done matters more than what they have not done.

The second reason why it is important to appreciate all you have done is that any runner's career can be over in a short space of time due to serious injuries. Welsh marathon legend Steve Jones famously said he was only ever a hamstring tear away from oblivion. This may sound like an exaggeration, but he is right. We can only run as long as our bodies cooperate and have the physical ability to do so. When I was training and racing well, I felt invincible, like there was no end to my capacity to train hard and compete at a high level. I noticed how few athletes who were over 40 competed at world level, but somehow when things were going well, it felt like it would never end. I thought I had many years ahead to race the marathon and aim for global championships. Inevitably, it was not like that. We all have a limited number of years of good running in us, especially at elite level. The physical wear and tear build up and the mental effort at elite level is not sustainable long-term. It is finite and fleeting, so why spend it dwelling on what you have not done? Life is short and embracing everything you can do along the way is vital. Of course, many athletes continue competing for many years, decades even. Their longevity is awe-inspiring. But for most of us, it is not like that. My advancement into middle age and the sudden realisation of probably being past the halfway point, certainly focused my mind on appreciating what I have done!

While I was competing, I had a tendency to think too much about what had not gone well. Perhaps it is only natural to notice the gaps, if there are any, between your plans and what you actually managed to do. I think it's fair to say that runners can often be unsatisfied! Yet running has so much going for it, including improved mental and physical health, social contact, and being out in the fresh air. It calls for all sorts of good attributes which can only help us in our non-running lives, including commitment, planning ahead, and the ability to work hard. So why not celebrate all that is positive about running? This was another area that sports psychologist Sarah Cecil helped me to look at in detail and the work she tasked me with was invaluable.

Sarah encouraged me to write down lists of anything and everything positive that I had accomplished. This act of recording – sitting down, pen in hand and thinking about all I had done that was positive – was a simple but brilliant piece of advice. It was an opportunity to remind myself of how hard I had worked, reflect on all the training I had completed, and feel confident about my preparations for a big race. I kept these lists and returned to them now and again when I was feeling low or was struggling in training. I tried to include everything that helped me with a race performance, not only training. It is easy to focus entirely on training and overlook or neglect the non-training elements of running, but the latter are as important and writing them down serves to highlight this. A typical list might include: completed quality long runs as planned, wore in racing shoes, practised running in race-day uniform, updated anti-doping whereabouts information on time, booked blood test, checked race start procedures, reduced weight down to race weight in good time, practised drinking on long runs, drank recovery drink immediately after all speed sessions, acclimatised to hot conditions, practised change of pace in steady runs, fulfilled obligations to sponsors, took rest days completely off training, bought blackout curtains to improve sleep and stretched for 30 minutes per day. When you see the extent of your efforts written down, it makes you feel good about yourself!

> **Make the best of all you have done. Record and appreciate it. Embrace the positive impact it will have on performance. Let go of what you haven't done.**

Insight 14
Nothing I Can Do

When training for a major marathon, I always prepared for the weather that was most likely on race day and took steps to be prepared for all weathers. Immediately before the 2007 Osaka World Championships and 2008 Beijing Olympics, I spent two weeks at home in Tokyo gradually acclimatising to hot and humid weather. I started training very early in the morning, while it was still cool. As I acclimatised, I trained later in the day. In essence, I exposed myself to hot and humid weather gradually, which allowed time for adjustment without risking dehydration or excessive fatigue. In Osaka, the temperature was 30 degrees at the start at 7 a.m., and 31 degrees at the finish. The humidity was high throughout. Thanks to thorough heat acclimatisation, I felt fine during the race and my performance was not affected by the hot weather. In Beijing, the weather was unexpectedly cooler than anticipated because of heavy rain two days before the women's marathon. I was well-prepared for hot weather but ran too conservatively given the actual weather on the day. Exceptionally challenging weather can be a positive opportunity if you have taken steps to prepare for it. It is a great leveller. Athletes who ordinarily would be expected to do well in favourable conditions often falter, leaving the way open for other athletes to shine.

The weather is only one factor which runners cannot control, but there are others, such as: travel delays, event cancellations and selection policies. All can be frustrating, but there is little, perhaps nothing, you can do to change them. It is easy to quickly fall into a negative spiral of disappointment, blaming others and giving up on your goals when factors which are out of your control go wrong. All your hard work going to waste makes you feel helpless. But there is something positive you can do in these situations. First, minimise the time and effort you spend on what you cannot control. Second, anticipate and prepare for scenarios in which things go wrong as constructively and positively as you can. Throughout my running career, I always tried to do this. It did not always work out as planned, but that was my aim. Selection policies are often the cause of frustration and disappointment for athletes. Controversies about athletes not being selected when they arguably should be blow up frequently. But however much you may disagree with how policies are written or decisions taken, it may not be possible to change them. You may have no choice but to accept them as they are and prepare accordingly. When I was aiming for selection onto teams for major events, I saw the heartache this process often caused. I decided to do my absolute best to avoid any such scenarios.

My approach to making teams was always to understand the selection policy as early as possible and to run a qualifying time as near to the start of the qualification period as I possibly could. If you can secure for yourself a position in which selectors are compelled by the policy to select you, it gives you confidence and frees up time and energy to concentrate on the main event. Once a selection policy is published, even if you disagree with it, the onus is on you to deliver what is called for. Appeals are different and often warranted if decisions appear to be objectively unfair or inconsistent with the policy. I lived for most of my elite marathon career in Japan. Gaining selection onto Japan's national team for any major championship marathon is exceptionally difficult. It is possibly the hardest national marathon team to get onto in the world. The standard of competition and depth is mind-bogglingly high. By comparison, making British marathon teams is relatively easy. I often reminded myself of this. To be brutally honest, if I were Japanese, I probably would never have raced in a global championship. I am always grateful for small mercies!

Minimising the time and effort you spend on things you cannot control is sensible. But I find this difficult when it comes to doping. Let's say I'm good at preaching, but not so good at practising! I can't control what other athletes do and yet it is difficult to ignore doping and its consequences. The scale of injustice associated with doping is sometimes staggering. The amount of fraud, exploitation of athletes, misleading of fans and sponsors, conflicts of interest, looking the other way, enabling of doping, and much else is extraordinary. Doping can rob clean athletes of medals, places in finals, prize money, qualification for major events, selections, confidence, self-belief, recognition, opportunities in retirement, and more. This is stating the obvious and is well known, but it is worth reminding ourselves from time to time of how challenging it is to preserve clean sport. I frequently become angry reading about doping but have accepted now that this is corrosive and unhelpful. Doping will never disappear altogether. It will ebb and flow, depending on how effective the dopers and anti-dopers are, relative to each other, at any given time. My advice to young athletes is to open your eyes and inform yourself thoroughly about doping and then focus on yourself and be the best you can be.

While training and competing in Japan, I grew to deeply respect Japanese athletes for how hard they trained and devoted themselves to their sport. But on top of that, they always respected their sport, their competitors and the field of play. Japanese athletes often cross the finish line and turn and bow towards the marathon course they have completed. I can't think of a single instance of underhand, unfair, or devious behaviour among the athletes and teams that I met. When Japanese athletes have been beaten in major marathons in Japan by athletes who were subsequently banned, I've felt so sad for them. These races are huge national events, broadcast live, often nationwide, and followed by millions of adoring fans on the streets and on television and radio. It is hard to overstate what a win by a Japanese athlete in one of these events means.

Let go of what you cannot control, however difficult that may be. Focus instead on preparing for unlikely and challenging scenarios.

Insight 15
Freedom to Flourish

One week after moving to Japan for the second time, in February 2006, I ran in the Kagawa Marugame International Half Marathon in Shikoku. I had been busy with packing up in London, moving home and country, and saying farewells to friends, family and colleagues, while trying to keep my training on track. One week after arriving, I still had jetlag so all in all, I was not keen on racing. But Shige convinced me to race and I am so glad that I did, and thankful to him for persuading me. It was an unforgettable experience. I finished third, with a new personal best of 69:24. But the best part of this race was sitting next to the then Olympic marathon champion, Mizuki Noguchi, at the presentation ceremony afterwards. She had finished second, behind the winner, Kayoko Fukushi, who had set an Asian record. I was sitting next to the Olympic champion! I was utterly awestruck by Noguchi, even though she is the smallest runner I have ever met – I am only 162cm tall but I towered over her. I was aiming for the 2008 Beijing Olympics, and there I was, not that far behind the Olympic champion in a half marathon. It gave me the biggest confidence boost I have ever experienced.

Two weeks later, I raced the Ohme Road Race 10km, the smaller cousin of the historic and hilly 30km race, which has long-standing links with the Boston Marathon. Compared to running a half marathon, 10km felt like a sprint and I ran another personal best of 31:43. In March, I ran in the Commonwealth Games 10,000m and won the bronze medal, which was totally unexpected. I then ran a personal best at the London Marathon in April of 2:25:13, moving up to second on the UK all-time list. These races were among the best I ever ran and much of that was down to how I felt mentally. The following aspects are what made them so special.

1. I was a newcomer to the Japanese running world, knew little about the Japanese athletes, and it was all exciting and new. The weight of past performances and expectations was non-existent.

2. Living in Japan, I was far away, physically, from anyone back in the UK who would take any notice. I could run freely and unhindered by any pre-conceptions about which Brits were on form, at what distance, which races, etc.
3. At the Commonwealth Games and London Marathon, I focused on myself and my own race. This was because I was well down the field on both start lists and needed an exceptional performance not to be left way behind. By focusing on myself, I managed to avoid being side-tracked by peripheral distractions.
4. In all these races, I did not pay too much attention to any splits or the pace. Instead, I just raced, trying to hang on for as long as possible, and then simply keeping it together and limiting the damage in the latter stages when I was really suffering.

We all create barriers in our minds for various reasons. We humans have evolved with strong instincts for survival. But along with those instincts come emotions, such as fear, which sometimes hold us back. How you handle these emotions has a huge impact on what you can achieve. If you find yourself in circumstances and an environment which liberate you mentally and enable positive performances, as I described above, make a note of it.

My score card on this during my running career has been mixed. In contrast to the events listed above, during the latter years of my career, the weight of expectation, advancing years, and injuries together made me mentally much weaker than in the earlier years. For most of us, there are scenarios in which we feel constrained, limited and frustrated by mental barriers.

How do you deal positively with mental barriers? Along the way, I learned invaluable habits to reduce their impact, or to eliminate them altogether. The following are examples of mental barriers I have encountered, with suggestions of something more positive that could replace them.

1. Running speed being determined by GPS watches and a set pace. Alternative: leave your watch at home, run at a variety of efforts, and see how it feels.
2. Compulsively comparing yourself with race performances from the past. Alternative: enter a race you have never done before, in a new place and over an untried distance. Or try a trail or cross-country race where time does not matter.

3. Becoming anxious or bewildered by the hype, media and social media interest in a forthcoming event. Alternative: write a to-do list for the week leading up to the race and write a schedule of when you will complete all the tasks on it. Stay off social media.
4. Feeling excessive pressure from yourself or others about an upcoming race. Alternative: focus on your process goals and perform them as best you can. Regardless of the result, you can walk away knowing that you could not have done better.
5. Fear about not achieving a goal you have set yourself. Alternative: use distraction techniques to think about something else or focus on improving your sleep.

When I think about mental barriers, three distinct features stand out. First, no incredible achievement, in any field, is quick or easy. If you look back through history, music, the arts, science, sport … every significant milestone was achieved step by step. Every expert, champion or inventor must start somewhere and build up. It is the same with running. Small forward steps over time make achievable what may initially seem impossible. Mental barriers can be broken down by making progress one small step at a time.

Second, activities and experiences which give you confidence are so valuable. For example, meeting people you look up to, experiencing difficulty but in small amounts, or learning about something before attempting it yourself. Meeting Mizuki Noguchi at Marugame made me realise that Olympic champions are just ordinary people who work exceptionally hard. Running longer training sessions than I had ever done before made me realise that they were actually possible – 10km tempo, 5 x 1km intervals, 10km tempo was the most epic session imaginable, until I did it.

Third, often the hardest step in taking on a big challenge is the first. In your head you might spend hours, days, weeks, months, years even mulling over how hard or impossible it might be. Before you know it, you will have created a wall of mental barriers which stops you from doing anything. It is better to simply start, with even the most modest of steps. The act of doing so will chip away at that wall. I often built a wall in my head before long runs. The thought of suffering through 35 or 40km built up in front of me, fear and anxiety increased, and motivation and willingness dwindled. Therefore, I told myself instead that it was only 5km, followed by another 5km, then another and another. That made me leave the house and start, by which time it did not seem quite so bad.

Mental barriers are entirely normal. Acquiring the ability to handle them is a skill which can be learned with self-awareness. Breaking them down is incredibly liberating.

Time for another drink

Part Four

Work With Others

Photo by Clive Rose/Getty Images

Insight 16
Confidence in Your Convictions

In June 2011, I had to decide whether to undergo surgery on my hamstring to resolve a high hamstring tendinopathy. My nickname for this injury was a 'pain in the bum' because that, literally, is what it was. Sitting down for a prolonged amount of time was painful and long car journeys could be unbearable. I had completed six months of rehabilitation but the injury was persisting. I was advised that surgery was the next logical option. However, I had strong instincts that told me this was not the right course of action. I was aiming for the London Olympics, so between July 2011 and April 2012, only nine months, I would have to recover from surgery, regain my fitness, run a qualifying time, and earn selection for Team GB. Shige and I had devoted years of our lives to me competing at London 2012. It was clear to me that nine months was too short and I would miss the Olympics. Therefore, I listened to my instincts and decided against surgery, in favour of trying a different approach to rehabilitation. This was not an easy decision. The people advising me were all highly-trained specialists. I wondered if it was foolish to go against their advice. In the end, my decision and the new approach bore fruit and I earned selection for London 2012 in early December 2011. I was very relieved that I had stuck to my guns.

Runners of all levels interact with other people such as coaches, teammates, club members, medical practitioners and others. None of us pursues this sport in isolation. All those people may have advice for you, as in the example above. At the same time, runners have to make decisions all the time – about what training to do, how to deal with injuries, planning races, choosing footwear, and so much more. What advice do you listen to, take on board and use? My approach to this was always: listen to different sources of advice; think carefully about whether or how this applies to you; and trust your instincts to make a decision that you believe serves you best. I encourage you to take the same approach with this book. Read my advice and decide carefully whether it is useful to you or not. I promise I won't be offended if it isn't!

Early on in my elite career, most of the information Shige and I gained was from our own initiative. We had to seek out knowledge and information and find our own answers to questions. I was a developing athlete, had no sponsors and was not on any support schemes. Our training programme was hard but included the top priority elements and was focused on the marathon. We had a clear roadmap to follow. Away from training, we tried our best to optimise process goals on everything else – food, rest, self-care and injury-prevention. Our simple regime worked well and I improved steadily. Life was simple!

As I became faster, people started to want to help us. This was gratifying. I was becoming good enough to attract the attention of people who offered support. The sportswear manufacturer Asics was one of the first. The first box of kit they sent me in 2005 was like a hundred Christmases all rolled into one! I put on the full race kit in our living room – racing crop top and briefs, sunglasses, headband, gloves, arm warmers, socks and racing shoes – the identical kit to what Constantina Dita had worn when finishing second at the London Marathon a few weeks earlier. Dressing up in the special kit of a world-class athlete felt magical.

Nobody wants to pass up offers of help when you are working hard at something. But as time went by, I had more and more people wanting to help. I was grateful, but I was spending a lot of time and effort trying to judge: What was likely to be helpful or not? Were these offers things I really needed or not? And was I able to provide what was expected in return? All of this was time and effort not spent on the simple but effective regime I had previously been concentrating on. The more this continued, the more I started to realise that I could manage without many of these offers or that what I was expected to provide in return was too onerous. Being someone who finds it difficult to say 'no', I ended up with far too much advice and was overwhelmed by managing it all. The contrast between the level of detail in my training diaries from the early and later years is stark. Over time, they became excessively complicated and full of minutiae. How I wish I had kept things simple.

During all this time, I should have trusted my instincts more and had confidence in my judgements. I was too inclined to take on board everything that came our way as if it were the gospel. What is saddest now as I look back is that I did not recognise and appreciate how effective a routine we had in the early days. If I had, I would have been more able to say 'no' to the less helpful advice coming our way later.

I have seen this happening to other runners. They describe their own observations and analysis of, for example, an injury. These appear to be entirely sound, carefully thought-through, and based on facts. But they will have thrown all that away in favour of other advice from someone they regard highly, even if this advice is clearly in conflict with their own carefully considered views. Using your own mind and trusting your instincts is so vital to be able to make sense of the sea of information we find around us.

Confidence in your convictions is important, too, for being honest with yourself when trouble strikes. Positive thinking, or finding positives in everything, is a well-known and widely-used strategy for coping with difficulty. It is a valuable survival mechanism. Everyone suffers setbacks, illness and difficulties in their lives. Having the resilience to push through this and carry on is vital. But often during my career, during injuries or times when I struggled to perform well, I applied a veneer of positive thinking to what I knew deep down was a serious situation. It was simpler to pretend that everything was fine and press on. But this merely prolonged problems. I should have listened better to my instincts that told me it was serious, faced up to the problem and taken steps to solve it properly.

> **Have the confidence to use your intuition and trust your instincts about what is best for you.**

Insight 17
The Orbit of Brilliance

Being a member of the late Bob Parker's training group at Parkside was an unforgettable learning experience. I joined them in the autumn of 1995 when I moved to London to start graduate studies. Parkside was a women's club although Bob's training group included some men too. When I arrived at Parkside, the senior women had won a seventh consecutive team title at the English National Cross Country Championships. They won an eighth in 1996. Andrea Whitcombe, Katy McCandless and Alison Wyeth all won individual titles. It was the most awe-inspiring team, not only of fast individuals but in depth too. I was one of the slower runners when I joined. I remember numerous training sessions when I was desperately trying to hang on to the faster runners. Rubbing shoulders at training with these athletes whom I respected so much was very inspiring and uplifting. But it was also quite a levelling experience because we all simply had to work hard together and grind out Bob's training sessions. Eventually after many months, I slowly closed the gap on some of the faster runners.

Bob's training was hard and consistent. We ran hills on Monday evenings, with at least seventy minutes of the warm-up and cool-down and we ran track on Tuesday evenings. I remember Wednesdays for barely being able to climb the stairs because I was so tired. On Thursdays we ran road reps. On Saturdays we ran grass intervals on local school playing fields, or cross-country fartlek sessions in the woods above the Bannister track; and long runs on Sundays. Bob's favourite instruction as we were training was "just floa' 'em mate". We all had a laugh trying to figure out what this actually meant. I often think of this instruction when runners nowadays ask me what pace they should run intervals at.

Living and working in an environment in which you are surrounded by able, talented and brilliant people is a terrific way to learn. It makes you raise your game to keep up with them and exposes you to effective behaviours, which you can copy and learn from. Ideas flow freely and it inspires you to improve. When I worked at the Foreign Office there seemed to be no end to brilliant, clever people everywhere.

Being a member of a training group, in which you're one of the slower runners, is an example of such an environment. If you are always trying to keep up at the back of the group, and have someone ahead who you can aspire to beat, it will spur you on to greater things. Seeing what faster runners do on and off the track can really help to build confidence. Observing how they train and realising that sometimes you can do the same, or even better, is a revelation. Seeing brilliant people make mistakes and how they recover from them, put things right and make amends, is reassuring.

Clubmates, training partners and fellow team members can be great sources of learning. Being a good runner is about so much more than how you train. Turning up on time to training, being organised about travel, how you treat your teammates, what you eat and drink, ensuring kit is in good working order, completing a session no matter what – all these factors matter.

Surrounding yourself with able people also exposes you to 'unknown unknowns' – knowledge that you don't know and don't even know exists. If you don't know it exists, you can't seek it out and learn it, unless it crosses your path by chance. I discovered numerous nuggets of wisdom about running through spending time with runners who were better than me. I heard about anti-inflammatory emu oil from one of my faster training buddies; the benefits of fermented foods for gut health from Japanese athletes; and the value of strength and conditioning for endurance runners from various athletes. When I was a young student athlete in the early 1990s, the notion of distance runners benefitting from strength and conditioning did not seem to exist. Hanging out with not only faster runners, but runners taking an approach entirely dissimilar to your own and runners from other countries, exposes you to new ideas, different ways of doing things, and knowledge that until now may have been an unknown unknown.

One lesson I learned from observing Japanese athletes is to show respect for your sport, your rivals and the field of play. Behaviour such as always turning up a bit early to training, listening quietly when a coach is speaking, not leaving your belongings lying strewn about during training ... these small behaviours speak volumes about how an athlete views their sport and others involved in it. These examples may seem like unnecessary detail or unduly burdensome, but they convey a message that others see. They are generic attributes that are useful in all areas of life. Training and competing in Japan was an absolute eye-opener for me. Every time I raced or encountered a Japanese team training, I felt like I was learning huge amounts about all aspects of running. Spending time in such a professional, competitive and top-quality environment was exactly what I needed to develop as an athlete.

Of course, you don't have to surround yourself with brilliant people to commit to doing your absolute best. When I think back to my mistakes in running it leaves me wondering, what on earth was I thinking? When I was a student, I missed the start of races twice. How could I make such a basic mistake?! When I think about the junk food I have eaten and the healthy alternatives I could have eaten instead if I had planned ahead, it feels like so many opportunities missed. And the carelessness which has led to injuries and months away from training. Learning is a lifelong process and never stops!

Seek out and spend time with brilliant people if you want to learn quickly. In running, as elsewhere, the environments they create are a stimulus to improvement and full of opportunities.

Insight 18
Scepticism, Always

When I was an undergraduate my politics tutor, Dr. Nigel Bowles, gave me the following advice: "Don't believe everything you read in the newspapers." I remember being surprised by this at the time. The implication of what he said was that at least part of the content of newspapers was untrue. I was reluctant to think that journalists or others writing in newspapers wrote outright falsehoods and lies. With the benefit of a few more decades of living, I've learned that some of what appears in the media is indeed untrue. Now we are into the age of social media, conspiracy theories and politics by spin and slick communications, this is perhaps truer than it has ever been. I doubt that Nigel intended to give the message that the world is full of liars and scoundrels. Rather, he was encouraging me to engage in critical thinking. To assess objectively the information I had read, to consider whether it was likely to be true or not and to look carefully at the evidence. I am grateful to him for instilling in me the importance of thinking for yourself and bringing a healthy scepticism to information that comes your way.

Developing the ability to objectively judge information, assess evidence, and establish facts, is vital in all areas of our lives. It is as indispensable in running as it is in anything else. Runners are constantly being told what to do. Therefore, developing and applying critical thinking skills to what you hear, read and see about running is useful to help you wade through all the information about it.

Let's look at examples from the running world. Many GPS watches can tell your VO_2 max score. As described in Insight 6, VO_2 max is a measure of the maximum amount of oxygen your body can use. GPS watches do not measure oxygen in any form. The only data about you that they can use is what you have inputted while setting up the watch and the training you have done while wearing it. You may not ever have run at your maximum, eyeballs out, top speed while wearing the watch. So how on earth can such a watch accurately measure your VO_2 max? These watches use data, such as heart rate, running speed, age and sex to calculate VO_2 max values.

Some of their estimates might be reasonably close to the true value. But these measures are never going to be a substitute for undergoing a lab-based test that measures oxygen uptake until exhaustion. Let's not throw the baby out with the bath water, but instead use these watch estimates with some healthy scepticism.

These are more examples of theories I have heard from runners that call for critical thinking.

1. A training programme consisting entirely of slow running will make you able to run fast in races.
2. Having a fast ground contact time will make you able to break three hours for a marathon.
3. Wiping sweat off your skin will help your body to cool down in hot conditions.
4. Taking supplements negates the need to eat any fruit and vegetables to stay healthy.

There may be some truth in these assertions. For example, there is a place in any training regime for slow running. It builds aerobic capacity and increases your total volume of training, which improves running economy and may help you to recover. A fast ground contact time is an outcome of having strong, robust and springy legs which might, among other things, make you run faster. I'm not dismissing these theories as totally redundant. But in and of themselves, they definitely call for questioning and probing to arrive at exactly how and why they might be useful.

Perhaps the part of the running world that calls the most for critical thinking is understanding the doping landscape. Fair and objective due process is always essential when someone may be accused of wrongdoing and consequently be required to serve a punishment. Similarly, we must assume that athletes are innocent until proven guilty. The official anti-doping organisations are the bodies responsible for enforcing anti-doping rules and catching doping athletes. But at the same time, critical thinking can serve to wake people up to what may be happening.

When the German investigative journalist Hajo Seppelt and his colleagues broke the news about Russian doping, extortion and cover-ups by the then International Association of Athletics Federations (IAAF) in 2014, it confirmed what I had suspected already: that some Russian female marathon runners were doping. People asked me how I was so sure. The answer is critical thinking and exactly what Nigel had told me to do – to not believe everything you see.

At the beginning of my career I knew that doping existed. But somehow the possibility of me lining up against dopers in the same race had not registered. I was naïve and cheerfully started every race on the assumption that it was a fair and honest competition. That changed over time as I competed in races in which there were aspects that simply did not make sense. I discussed this with my friends, which made clear how naïve I had been. I went through a real wake-up call, and decided to apply a healthy scepticism to everything I saw.

From 2006 onwards, I frequently raced against or observed athletes whose performances were, in some respects, baffling, including: athletes finishing marathons with absurdly fast closing splits yet looking very fresh; athletes breezing past world-class clean athletes apparently effortlessly; and athletes who clearly looked out of shape running exceptional performances. These performances left me puzzled. Even a small amount of questioning and thought led to the conclusion that something was not right. I reassured myself that action would be taken, that the relevant anti-doping authorities would investigate and catch any cheats. Years passed with apparently little change. I grew weary of having to line up in races against athletes who were producing absurd performances. This was a contributing factor in my eventual decision to retire.

I wrote a blog about critical thinking and doping in 2016, in which I encouraged readers to engage in a level of scepticism when they see an apparently spectacular performance. The searching questions I suggested readers ask themselves, when witnessing a supposedly amazing run are below.

1. When a performance does not make sense, leaves you baffled, or does not quite add up, ask yourself why and how?
2. Which country is an athlete from and what is the history of doping in that country? Does it have a fit-for-purpose anti-doping system?
3. Does the athlete's awesome performance make sense, considering their body type?
4. Is a lot of money at stake for the athlete, their entourage and others?
5. Who does the athlete spend time with and who is their coach and agent?
6. Are an athlete's performances consistent over time and across events? Has there been a sudden and big improvement?

7. What was the athlete's finish like? Did it look easy? Like they had a lot left in the tank?
8. Has the athlete been competing regularly? Where? Only in their own country?
9. Does the athlete look like they are training for their particular event and look fit, in shape, and ready to compete?

Critical thinking will serve you well in running and in other areas of life. Objective facts, compelling evidence and logical arguments are the foundation of truth. Be sceptical about anything that does not make sense.

Insight 19
Carry Others With You

When I was living in Japan, if we were going to a race away from Tokyo in a regional town or city, we always tried to visit a local school to give a talk or running class. I absolutely loved these visits. The children's enthusiasm and excitement were always so uplifting. Their questions kept me on my toes. The best question ever, which was from a primary school child was, "When you win a race, how much money do you get?" They were a good antidote to competing in a high-pressure race which involved mainly focusing on myself. These races and accompanying school visits took us to many corners of Japan and the insight into life outside Tokyo was wonderful. At a local level, people are so heart-warmingly proud of their home; relish giving warm and generous hospitality; and love welcoming outsiders to their neck of the woods. I have lived in Tokyo and London for all – except one year – of my adult life; you simply do not experience this atmosphere and culture in big cities in the same way. The sense of teamwork around these local running events was incredibly special.

Running is by nature a solitary, individual sport. When you line up on the start line of a race it's only you. It is you who has to train hard in all weathers. Running as a team sport, of course, also exists and is immensely popular but it's not always a team sport like football or rugby. You can run completely alone and many runners love that aspect of it – you can clear your head and have time to yourself.

Yet running is very much a team effort, certainly at elite level. Every elite athlete depends on the support of a team around them. It's difficult to train and compete at a high level without this. This team might include: family members, training partners, one or more coaches, a physiotherapist, a nutritionist, a doctor, an agent, and others. Unfortunately, when you see an athlete performing at a major competition or on television, the extent of that support often is not clear.

Bringing supporters and teammates along with you is all important – as it is in work and all walks of life. If others are helping you, it is vital to recognise their support, motivate them, lead by example, show you value them, and be thankful for their efforts. I always tried my best to do this but regret that the physical and mental demands of training and competing often meant I was not doing it anywhere near enough, or as well as I would have liked to. But committing to doing your best in bringing others along with you is a valuable learning experience, no matter how good you are at it in the end.

I am eternally grateful to all the people who provided support to me so I could train and compete as an elite athlete. There were many and I am so thankful for their patient, selfless and dedicated hard work. There is no doubt that without their help, I would not have been able to train and compete as I did.

Nobody helped me more than Shige. I would never have been able to live the life of an elite athlete without his help. Without me asking, he started helping me in the early days in a number of ways by: teaching himself from scratch all about marathon running; transforming my performance on non-training elements including nutrition, self-care and race preparation; and helping with day-to-day tasks such as, accompanying me to training, cooking meals, doing massage, supermarket shopping and more. I have seen numerous people tell others to be good at something without actually helping, but Shige did the everyday things that I needed help with.

Later, he became my coach, agent and manager. On top of all the above, he negotiated with races; organised travel to races and training camps; sought, negotiated and agreed contracts with sponsors; managed all my appearances; came to nearly every training session and race; and did many of the daily domestic tasks at home. All of this he did selflessly, patiently and always to the best of his ability. The huge amount Shige did for me was mostly unseen by others. He did everything to an exceptionally high standard but never bragged about it and was always modest. Sadly, people like this are often underappreciated and their hard work goes unrecognised. I am ashamed that he was criticised about how he spent his time. Many people have little idea about the amount of effort and sheer hard work that goes into elite sport, from the athlete themselves but also from their support team. I was extremely fortunate to have received Shige's help over many years and am very grateful for it. My elite career would not have happened without it.

At recreational level, the team aspects of running are so fundamental. Now that I am retired and running again at this level and coaching recreational runners, I appreciate these aspects more.

1. Runners of all levels and abilities are role models to people around them, often without realising it. At Woolacombe Dunes parkrun, I saw three generations of the same family all participating and providing inspiration to other families. I also met a small boy, who had completed 70 parkruns, though he was only seven. When I congratulated him, he didn't seem to think it was a big deal. He was setting such a brilliant example to other children and indeed the adults around him.

2. If you're a member of a regular training group, the pain and hard work you go through together with your training buddies, week in and week out, is a bonding experience like no other. You suffer and go through hard times together, but also improve, find inspiration and help each other together.

3. Running is a great leveller across ages and backgrounds, and it bonds people who otherwise may have little in common. The wealthiest, most brilliant business executive becomes the same as anyone else when they line up on a race start line. Money, prestige, status, class, privilege and any other advantage will not make you run fast without hard work. Running breaks down social and economic barriers between people.

4. Running is often defined in terms of speed. But runners who may not be the fastest are often those who are fundamental to enabling and delivering our sport – as volunteers, team managers, coaches and officials. These people are as vital as anybody in enabling us all to enjoy running.

Paying attention to bringing others along with you can help to dilute the inevitable aspects of running being an individual sport, such as runners being a bit inward looking or obsessive about their own training and performances. I am very guilty of this! I honestly admit that I can become fixated on running, excessively competitive and obsessed by minutiae of my own running. None of these tendencies is attractive as a personal attribute. I am often embarrassed, even ashamed, about them. I think a few runners have these tendencies and there is even a name for it – 'the running bore'! In a way, distance running self-selects for these attributes. You have to be a bit obsessive to readily put yourself through the pain of large amounts of training.

When you toe the start line in a running race, you are there by yourself. Even if you're part of a team, the section you have to run is down to you alone. It is very individual and can be lonely. But this is not always healthy. Lifting yourself out of this individualised world and seeing the impact you are having on people around you is vital. Of all the insights in this book, this is the one that I wish I had worked at much harder.

Even in a solitary activity there is always a team element. Always do your best to support, encourage and motivate people around you.

Insight 20
Coaching

Coaches are only human and do their best, but they have their shortcomings like everybody else. During the years while I was a member of Bob Parker's group, I absolutely loved training, improved rapidly, and relished being part of a thriving group. Bob's approach was simple – sheer hard work. There was nothing fancy or scientific about it. We all ground out the sessions and helped each other. Because I was young, improving, and relatively new to organised, hard training, I never questioned Bob's coaching. I did exactly what he set without thinking much about it. But I did have a tendency to train too much and pack in too much racing. If I had a disappointing race, I was too quick to see it as his fault since he was in charge. After reflecting on this, I soon realised how unfair this was, and that I had to take responsibility for my own performances. This called for me to think more carefully about and take ownership of everything I was doing as an athlete – not the training that Bob was setting, but all the other areas including recovery, nutrition, looking after myself and injury-prevention. I understood that even though Bob was a terrific coach and was devoted to his runners like they were his family, ultimately, he could not do everything. My expectations of him were too high. I had to appreciate all he did for me and his other charges but make my own effort in other areas. In other words, my performances had to be a team effort by him and me.

Coaching is the bedrock of developing athletes in all sports. What I learned from experiencing and observing a variety of coaching over many years is that diversity in all aspects of coaching is valuable. One size does not necessarily fit all. What works for one athlete will differ from the next. The ultimate goal of coaching must be to optimise an athlete's performance, however that is best achieved.

I have been coached, mentored and helped informally by a number of coaches.

» My father, who in the early days helped me to stick with running long enough that my fitness improved and I started to enjoy it. By somewhat devious means he also persuaded me to join the cross-country club when I went to university. Despite his deviousness, I am eternally grateful to him for this.

» Julian Goater, who coached the student team at Oxford University and encouraged me to join Parkside when I moved to London. This brief conversation with Julian changed my life.

» The late Bob Parker, who ran the superb Parkside women's team from his home in North Harrow.

» Bud Baldaro and Alan Storey, from whose knowledge and experience in the marathon I learned a huge amount.

» Shige, who despite having no previous knowledge of distance running, taught himself everything about the marathon from scratch and left no stone unturned.

» Michael Woods, who provided invaluable help when I was qualifying as a coach and trying to extend my running career.

» Myself.

After retiring from elite competition in 2013, I qualified as an Athletics Coach under the system then offered by UK Athletics. I see this qualification as a basic platform on which to build knowledge and experience through lifelong learning. Since qualifying, I have coached runners of varying abilities, and have developed my views on coaching from behind the stopwatch, as it were. Over all these years, my observations boil down to the following points, which together spell the message that diversity in personalities, styles, backgrounds and approaches is valuable.

Communicating well, being able to motivate and instil self-belief are the fundamentals of good coaching, more than the nitty-gritty of what training athletes need to do. Naturally, the latter does matter – coaches must have a reasonable level of understanding of physiology, the effects of training and how adaptation works. But how a coach influences an athlete's mindset in a positive and encouraging way is paramount. This is akin to the effect that exceptionally gifted teachers have on children – setting them off on an upward trajectory that ultimately is driven by the individual, not the teacher.

I believe that you do not have to have been a world-class athlete to be a great coach. This notion simply seems unhelpful to me. First, it excludes a huge number of people whose skills and insights could enable them to become great coaches. Second, the nuts and bolts of coaching distance running can be learned, by reading and mining the numerous sources available. Shige coached me to finishing sixth in the Olympics with no background at all, by reading and learning from others. Third, in some ways I think being an elite athlete is poor preparation for being a good coach. Athletes are told what to do much of the time. Training is very repetitive. You spend a lot of time thinking about yourself. Your life revolves around you, not others. None of this is particularly helpful preparation for learning how to be a great motivator, how to communicate well, or how to really understand others' needs. Of course, former top athletes have a wealth of knowledge and experience about the content of training and racing. But transferring that knowledge effectively to another individual and replicating world-class success is not always straightforward.

My final observation is that the person who knows you the best is you and therefore, self-coaching can be, and often is, a great form of coaching. Ultimately, the person who must stand on the start line, put themselves through pain, and deliver the goods in races is the athlete, not the coach, however good the coach may be. Coaching yourself also forces you to learn about training, adaptation, racing, and so much more. As an athlete, understanding all of this will certainly serve you well. The benefits of self-coaching are as useful for recreational runners as for elite athletes. Using your brain, thinking carefully about your routine, and figuring out what works for you will certainly help you to improve more rapidly.

Towards the end of my career, I was effectively self-coached. I had accumulated enough knowledge, experience and self-awareness that I felt I was the best judge of what my routine should consist of. I am not claiming I knew everything, nor that there wasn't room or need for others' input. Certainly, my tendency to train excessively meant I probably would have benefitted from the views of somebody who was more detached and could take an outsider's overview. But after years of being coached by and learning from others, and remembering that it was me who had to suffer through 42.195km, I decided the most straightforward approach was to be my own coach.

A few years ago, I coached a one-off session for the staff at a large international company in central London. Before we started, I asked everyone to answer the questions, "I want to run because …" and "I like running because …" My session was a one-off and I wanted them to think a little about how they might continue running after my session. The answers were along the lines of, "I dislike my boss", "I feel stressed", "To get away from my wife", "I want something I can enjoy." I was quite taken aback. All the answers were about coping with difficulty. Not one of them said, "I love running" or "I want to improve." I thought for a moment and decided that, above all, this group needed fun and enjoyment. I abandoned any thoughts of performance, running fast, or good technique. Instead, I created a session which was simply fun.

Coaching must be about enabling good performance and instilling self-belief. There are a multitude of ways to achieve that.

Making good progress!

Part Five

Execute a Performance Well

Insight 21
Build Up or Down

When preparing for a major event away from running, the weeks immediately preceding the event are often the toughest phase when there is the most work to do. As deadlines loom, decisions need to be taken and time runs out – you have to complete all the necessary work, on time, ready for the big day. There is a build-up of effort as you approach the day itself. However, for the marathon, the opposite is true – you need to build down your effort to ensure you are fully rested and eager to perform at your best on race day. The same applies to other events which require a huge physical and mental effort, such as exams, interviews, or giving a speech to a large audience. This process, known as tapering, is perhaps the most important part of executing a performance well, even though it happens in advance of the performance. Its purpose is to make you arrive at the big day feeling mentally and physically on top of your game and raring to go.

Runners often ask me about tapering and how I did it: what training I did, over how many weeks and what kind of sessions I ran. I always answer these questions by returning to the purpose of a taper. What works for one person may be very different to another. The content of a taper will be influenced by what else is going on in a runner's life and how much spare time and energy that runner has. But whatever any one runner does during a taper, the result of it should always be the same: to make the runner feel fresh, rested, keen to race and chomping at the bit. It really doesn't matter what you do; if it makes you perform at your best, it works. It's important to not lose sight of this when thinking about the content of your taper.

The obvious items to include in a taper are activities which will help you to feel positive on race day: rest, sleep, looking after yourself, eating properly, good hydration, training, and race preparation. Similarly, anything which may or will detract from your performance needs to be avoided, if possible: long-haul air travel, stressful events at work, major life events like moving house, illness, injuries, risky activity like dangerous sports, food and drink which might make you feel ropey and excessive training.

My standard taper lasted for three weeks. I kept my training programme the same as normal, but reduced the total amounts to 80% of my usual volume in the first week, 50% in the second week and 30% during race week (excluding race day itself). For example, if I normally ran 10 intervals of 1 km, I ran eight in the first week of tapering. My last speed training was always on Wednesday or Thursday of race week. I often had Friday and Saturday completely off running. However, I often had to include other factors which disrupted this regime, for example, long-haul flights from altitude training camp venues, heat acclimatisation and obligations to the race such as press conferences. In all these cases, I adapted my standard taper as best I could to take account of these factors, while ensuring I arrived at the start line feeling up for racing. Three weeks is a long time and is the longest taper I have come across. Two weeks, or even one, is enough for many runners. If you have missed a large chunk of training during your preparation due to illness or injury, you can probably shorten your taper to provide more time for training.

Tapering before a marathon is the best time to try out marathon race pace. The race is coming around soon, so your fitness level will not change that much. Nearly all your hard training is done and the effects of it will be showing. Reducing your training means you will feel more rested, as you will on race day. Most importantly, you need to decide what pace you will aim for on race day, experience how this pace feels and make a judgement about whether you can maintain it for the whole marathon. I always included at least two efforts at my target marathon race pace while tapering. Occasionally during heavy training, I ran tempo efforts and was not able to hit my marathon race pace. This was very unsettling. If I could not run at marathon race pace for any distance, how would I do it for 42.195km? But always, the restful effect of tapering and the atmosphere on race day meant I managed to lift my performance to my target race pace.

In the final weeks before the 2005 London Marathon, I ran two efforts of 10km at marathon race pace on the course early on a Sunday morning. I was aiming for 2:32 to qualify for the Helsinki World Championships. But my times for these efforts were equivalent to 2:28 and I felt comfortable. This is a perfect example of how using marathon race pace can inform the process of finalising what pace you will set off at, whether that is faster or slower than what you had been planning. By doing these efforts, I discovered that I was in better shape than 2:32 and ran much of the race a little faster than that. In the end, I faded in the final stages and finished in 2:31:52. I believe this was due to lack of muscular endurance, rather than being too ambitious about my pace.

The most valuable tip I ever learned about tapering was to write it down. By doing so, I had a template which I could use, update, scrutinise and refer to for all future races. I had a model to follow, and never had to start from scratch again, deciding what to include. All this effort was useful miles in the bank.

A taper needs to make you feel raring to go on race day. The content doesn't matter. If it works for you, use it.

Check your watch!

Insight 22
Always Do Your Best!

Before the 2007 Osaka World Championships Marathon, I felt enormous pressure because it was a 'home' championship, and I had run a huge personal best of 68:45 at the Sapporo International Half Marathon a few weeks earlier, defeating Kenyan marathon legend Catherine Ndereba. I was in great form, despite having been ill two weeks before. I felt weighed down by this pressure and that anything less than a medal would not be good enough.

The early stages of the race were slow because of the heat and humidity. There remained a large group in contention well into the second half. I knew I didn't have the finishing speed of several of my rivals, so I wanted to move the race along well before the finish. Nobody was making any effort to do this, so I went to the front at around the 29km mark. I knew the course well and at this point it felt like we were well into the closing stages. But I increased the pace too fast and too soon and at about 32km, the now smaller lead group passed me. I hung on as best I could but ended up finishing in ninth place, which was definitely worse than I was capable of on that day. If I had simply done my best, without worrying so much about high expectations and medals, I believe I would have performed much better – perhaps not enough to win a medal, but certainly better than ninth. By overthinking the entire project, I excessively complicated it and misjudged my tactics. I did not deliver my absolute best in the end because pressure, high expectations and nerves derailed me.

When it comes to performing in a competition, it is self-evident that you should aim to do your best. This is competition after all – the opportunity to make use of all your hard work in training and see what you are capable of. Yet, so much seems to keep us from doing this simple task, much of it inside our own heads.

It's not difficult to do your best when things are going well. If you feel strong in a race, training has gone well and you know you are in shape, everything feels positive and you can relish delivering your absolute best.

However, it is an entirely different picture when you're struggling, for whatever reason. Setbacks can quickly lead you into a negative mindset and into the temptation to make excuses for not giving it everything. But this will make matters worse. It's easy to fall into a sequence of negative thoughts and decisions which may then result in a poor performance. It is absolutely vital to stop this process as soon as you can, but how?

When racing, I always tried to give my best, no matter the circumstances. It didn't always turn out that way, but this is what I aimed for. To do this, I used specific mental tricks, which reinforced my focus about simply giving it everything, as listed below.

1. Reminding myself of all the positive, hard work I had completed during my preparation.
2. Believing that the other athletes were suffering as much as I was.
3. Focusing on the here and now, to displace thoughts about how far away the finish was or what the result would likely be.
4. Setting myself little goals, such as reaching the next lamppost, mile marker or drinks station to maintain my concentration.
5. Trying to convince myself that it was not that hard by relaxing or breathing more slowly.

Which mental trick works will vary from one person to the next, so it's worth experimenting to find whatever helps you to maintain a positive mindset. Then, all you have to do is ... do it. If you can produce your absolute best in a race, no matter what, you can walk away regardless of the result feeling that you could not have given more.

Producing your level best often calls for pushing the boat out, going faster than you have ever run before and taking a leap into the unknown. If you're fitter than you have been recently or ever, by definition your best on that day will be a stretch beyond what you have run before. At the Tokyo International Women's Marathon in 2005, I ran through halfway much faster than ever before. But I felt comfortable, so despite it being a trip into unknown territory, I did not let the halfway split worry me. This is why I believe it is so valuable to sometimes run without your watch and free yourself to run hard, without any limits. As soon as you put a watch on, you will be tempted to run according to a set pace that has previously defined what your best is, or to check your watch as you go along. When you check your watch, your brain will then attempt to process that information, and that might not necessarily help your performance. Delivering your absolute best is about the greatest physical and mental effort you can produce at a given moment, not what your watch says.

Marathon running these days for most runners is effectively a time trial. Out of the thousands who start any marathon, only a tiny number have a chance of winning, overall or within a specific category. In a way, this is unfortunate because racing is a different beast altogether from running a time trial, and a terrific vehicle for pushing yourself to your absolute limits. At a talk I gave a few years ago, a member of the audience explained that his next goal was to win a marathon. His personal best was about 2:45 and he had deliberately chosen a race which was usually won in around that time. He was not interested in the finish time, he simply wanted to win. I thought this was brilliant! He had set himself a challenging and exciting but realistic goal, which pushed him much more than merely running a time trial. This made me realise that in my own marathon career, I too often competed in races that realistically I had a slim chance of winning. With hindsight I regret this now. I wish, especially early on, I had chosen slightly lower quality marathon races, and set out to win them. By genuinely attempting to win, you develop invaluable racing skills, and that builds confidence.

I finished the 2007 World Championships knowing that I hadn't delivered my best. Tempering my disappointment on that day was the incredible performance of Japan's Reiko Tosa, one of the best marathon races I have ever seen. This was the final day of the championships and the hosts Japan had not yet won a medal. In the final few kilometres, she was on her own in fourth place, well behind third. By this time the sun was fully up and it was 31 degrees Celsius. Somehow through gritted teeth, Tosa clawed her way back to the Chinese athlete ahead of her, overtaking her to finish third. Without doubt, this was an example of simply doing your absolute best on race day.

> **Give your best, whatever level that is, when it matters. This is a skill which can be learned.**

Insight 23
Use Mistakes

My one and only marathon victory was in January 2008, in the Osaka International Women's Marathon. This was one of Japan's top races for elite women. What made this win so special was that I managed to avoid repeating the costly mistake I had made five months earlier, on the same course at the Osaka World Championships. I learned from that experience and used much better tactics. The redemption was sweet!

At the World Championships, as described in the last Insight, I surged too fast and too early, faded in the final stages, and finished a disappointing ninth. In January 2008 when I returned to Osaka, I was definitely going to hold something back for the final few kilometres and avoid the temptation to surge too early. Japan's queen of the track, Kayoko Fukushi, set off well inside 2:20 pace on her marathon debut. There was no way I could sustain that pace so I let her go, as did everyone else. I felt comfortable in the first half. The race even felt too slow and I wanted to push on, but I resisted and simply tried to expend as little energy as possible. All the while there was no sight of Fukushi who was way ahead.

At about 30km, the racing started to get underway and the pace gradually crept up. But this was close to where I had taken off too early the previous year. I stayed with the group. Without even attempting a surge, a few kilometres farther on, I found myself on my own at the front. I had gradually dropped the rest of the group. I had not injected a sudden change of pace so was not suffering unduly. *I am on my own and have dropped the others,* was all I could think. I simply tried to hold the gap and gradually apply pressure. Soon, the television trucks came into view and I realised they were accompanying Fukushi. For the first time ever in a marathon I thought, *I can win this*. That realisation was electric! The gap to Fukushi was closing fast so I knew she must be really struggling. I caught her and went into the lead. From then on, I focused entirely on simply surviving, holding my nerve and maintaining the gap. Running into Nagai stadium onto the track for the final three hundred metres, leading the marathon was the best experience of my life. It was all the sweeter because it was a form of redemption after the mistakes of the previous summer.

The only disappointment from that day was I soundly defeated Constantina Dita who went on to become Olympic Champion seven months later.

However unpleasant it is when you mess up, have a disappointing performance, or fail at something, at least these experiences can lead to learning. Nobody is perfect; we all make mistakes. It is inevitable. You can't lead an active and full life without sometimes messing up. Running is the same – sometimes you will train or race way below your ability, for whatever reason.

What is absolutely vital in running, to improve over time, is to avoid making the same mistakes over and over, and to be honest with yourself about why you have messed up. If you can quickly identify the reason for the mistake, you can set about rectifying it and avoiding a repeat. There may be reasonable explanations for poor performance. I have run disappointing races because of low iron – a legitimate reason for feeling ropey, but it was definitely a mistake not to be on top of this beforehand by having a blood test.

When identifying causes, it's useful to ask yourself searching questions. Was it something that has become chronic, like having low self-confidence? Was it something unrelated to running, like having a stressful week at work? Was this the first instance of poor performance, or is there a pattern? Objectively and honestly identifying the causes of your mistakes and addressing them is helpful. Something like being busy at work can be mitigated next time by taking a day's leave in the run-up to a race. Anything related to practical areas like kit, drinks, and travel really must be ironed out through experimenting and being well organised. It's a shame to allow mistakes on practicalities to put your hard work in training to waste.

In 2011, I was faced with repeating a mistake I had previously made, but this time I did not have much choice. In the 2008 Tokyo International Women's Marathon, I desperately wanted to win. The organisers had decided to discontinue this event so the 2008 race was the final edition. British marathon pioneer Joyce Smith had won the first edition in 1979 and the second in 1980. I wanted to join Joyce in 'book-ending' this race by being a British winner of the final race. I was disappointed at missing out on the medals at the Beijing Olympics and believed I was fast enough to win this race. But on the day, the top Japanese athletes set off at a blistering pace and I was never at the front for any length of time. I could only race at what for me was a sensible pace and hope the others would pay for it later.

Sure enough, into the second half, I started catching the runners up front. I could see Yoshimi Ozaki up ahead; the gap was closing fast so I thought she must be fading rapidly. I expected to breeze past – I didn't think I needed to give her a wide berth, which would make it more difficult for her to tag on to me. But as I drew level, she tucked in behind me and started following me. I was surprised by this because I had caught her so quickly. I kept trying to drop her, but she clung on. In the final few kilometres, she dropped me and produced a sensational finish to win the race. I was mad at myself for letting her use me as a pacemaker and helping her win. In the final stages, I managed to catch one of the early leaders, Yoko Shibui, and finished third. It was so disappointing to think that I had run with the eventual winner for a huge chunk of the second half, helping her along. All because I made the mistake of trying to pass her, right next to her. I resolved never to repeat this mistake again.

Fast forward to November 2011 and I was racing in the Yokohama Women's Marathon trying to qualify for the London 2012 Olympics. I had to run about 2:27 to gain pre-selection in December 2011. This race was much more about the time rather than where I finished, so I tried to run my own race, aiming for 2:27. I had not run at all between January and June 2011 due to injury so was not at all confident of my form.

At about halfway, the lead group slowed right down and I caught up with them. The mistake I had made in Tokyo 2008 was clear in my memory and I really didn't want to repeat it by becoming a pacemaker for this group. But the pace kept slowing and I was starting to risk missing my goal time of 2:27. I couldn't waste more time deciding, so I went to the front of the group and ended up being the pacemaker again. I regretted making that mistake again. But this time, my main goal for this race was to qualify for the Olympics, which meant my finishing time was the top priority. I did not, in practice, have a choice. Despite being a pacemaker again, I ran 2:27:24, finishing third and securing early selection. Job done.

As in the 2007 Osaka World Championships, ahead of me one of the most extraordinary performances I have ever seen was unfolding. Tokyo winner Ozaki was going for another win and dropped Ryoko Kizaki in the final kilometres. She built up an apparently unassailable lead and the race looked like it was over. But Kizaki somehow fought back, closed the gap and won. There are few better examples of phenomenal marathon racing than Kizaki's final effort.

We all make mistakes. They are part of living a full life. By identifying why they happen, we can learn from them and improve.

Insight 24
What Is the Worst?

It's natural to feel anxious before a marathon or some other big challenge you have taken on. Anxiety is useful because it galvanises you for the task ahead. It makes you focus and be ready to deliver a huge physical and mental effort. But excessive nerves are not helpful because they may have detrimental effects on you: mental exhaustion, being unable to think clearly, or reluctance to take on what lies ahead.

For many people, the source of nerves may be quite irrational. We might become nervous about small, inconsequential things which, in the grand scheme of things, do not matter. It is sometimes useful to look way, way back to what humans originally had to be worried about, namely, survival. Millennia ago, there was good reason to be anxious and to have your fight-or-flight response triggered if you were about to be attacked by predators or lose your life in some other way. Nowadays, we rarely face the prospect of possibly losing our lives, but other factors set off our fight-or-flight response. Therefore, finding ways to manage anxiety levels is indispensable and is always time and effort well spent.

Sports psychologist Sarah Cecil taught me how to dispel anxiety by embracing the worst. If I was feeling nervous before a major race, she suggested I write down the worst that could happen. Having done that, I was to think about each scenario – what exactly would happen, what I would do about it and how I could turn it into a positive. This proved to be an extremely helpful exercise for putting my worries into perspective.

Top of the list of the worst that could happen while I was preparing for a marathon is ... death! This was very unlikely to happen. If it did, there was nothing I could do about it anyway. I didn't spend too much time on that scenario. The next worst possibility was being unable to start the race due to injury, accident, or illness. After thinking about this, I decided it would be disappointing, possibly costly financially, and I would have to rearrange my race plans. But none of this was life-threatening, and life would go on. Next was starting, but not being able to finish the race.

Again, that would be disappointing, but life would go on. Then there was finishing the race, but after a poor performance. I would be disappointed, embarrassed and frustrated, but again life would continue. The more I imagined all these disparate scenarios, the more I realised that none of them was particularly serious. The world would not end, I would regroup and find a new challenge. This realisation felt liberating, and none of what might possibly happen seemed that bad. I understood that I was becoming anxious about trivial matters, which was a complete waste of mental energy before a big race.

After thinking through various worst-case scenarios, Sarah also encouraged me to imagine more nuanced scenarios that could nevertheless detract from an otherwise good performance. For example, what if I am in the lead in the final stages? What if I fall over? What if I set off and feel terrible? What if I am not on course to reach my goal? What if I miss one of my drinks? What if someone invades or obstructs the course? What if it rains heavily? Before the start of the 2012 London Olympics Marathon there was an almighty downpour! The list of possible scenarios is long. Having written a list, Sarah asked me to think about how I would feel and react. Unlike the worst-case scenarios, which were mostly about damage limitation, some of these scenarios had potentially good outcomes.

This made me focus on the positive outcomes to such scenarios. The process of imagining these good outcomes made them feel familiar and comfortable. I no longer feared any of these scenarios because I knew that if any happened I was ready for them and could react quickly. In essence, this exercise was about training myself to deliver a positive outcome from a scenario which could go either way.

In the final laps of the 2006 Commonwealth Games 10,000m, I was in no-man's land in fourth place. This was exactly such a scenario. I could have finished out of the medals or winning a bronze medal. But strangely this situation was precisely what I had visualised while training in the weeks leading up to that race. I remember running 20 x 400m repetitions in the Tokyo National Stadium in February 2006. It was a fabulous stadium and even had cold and hot baths in the changing rooms – this was the highlight I looked forward to after sessions there! I was alone on the track and imagined a TV commentator talking about me winning the bronze medal. It was a bit of light relief that helped me to complete the session. This is exactly what did happen in Melbourne. Being within striking distance of the bronze medal was familiar territory in my imagination, so instinctively I knew immediately how to react.

When I was preparing for the 2008 Osaka International Women's Marathon, I used Sarah's advice to imagine a variety of worst-case and unpredictable scenarios. Yet on the day, something happened which I had not foreseen. As we approached one of the drinks stations in the middle of the race, I sighted my bottle and reached out to grab it. I caught it safely and ran on. But to my alarm, I discovered I had someone else's bottle hanging from my arm! Many of the Japanese athletes put wire hoops on their bottles to make them easier to catch. When a large group approaches a drinks station, inevitably there is barging and confusion, so anything which makes your bottle easier to catch is worth trying. As I went to grab my bottle, I had inadvertently put my arm through the hoop attached to another bottle without seeing it. I had to act fast, so I removed the bottle from my arm and threw it back to the drinks station, calling to the officials that I had caught it by mistake. I wondered afterwards if I should have gone back, but I would have lost touch with the group. It was a genuine mistake and I made an effort to rectify it. I never discovered whose bottle it was.

> **Imagining a variety of scenarios, particularly the worst, makes them familiar and therefore easier to handle. This helps with grasping positive outcomes from difficult situations.**

Insight 25
Perfect on Practicalities

When preparing for a marathon, being on top of all the practical and logistical aspects is essential and an easy win. There are a multitude of decisions to make and details to organise. This might feel like a burden when you want to focus your energy on training. But in my experience, this is always effort well spent, for a number of reasons.

First, you will have to make decisions about practicalities at some point. Therefore, why not make them in good time, when you can think carefully about them, not be rushed, and make sound decisions. This will free up mental energy on race day for devoting to your performance and running fast. For me, the knowledge that all the practical aspects were in order and well organised gave me confidence on race day and reduced anxiety. Not having to spend any time or energy on decisions had a calming effect on me. Further, organising practicalities in good time meant I could refine, correct and adjust anything with which I was not happy.

Second, race day and during the race itself are not good times to be making important decisions. The nerves of race day, the lack of time available and the effect of carbohydrate depletion on the brain are all likely to impair rather than enhance your ability to make decisions.

Third, this is an area in which you can steal a march on your rivals. If your fellow competitors are sloppy in their preparation but you are well organised, that might contribute to you running faster than them. Without doing any more training, or being a better athlete than your rivals, this allows you to have an advantage over them. The results of marathons run in extreme weather can be determined entirely by how well or not each athlete has prepared for such conditions.

Fourth, if you have trained hard for a marathon, it's a pity to allow poor organisation to diminish your performance and allow your hard work to go to waste. When practicalities go wrong in a marathon, there is plenty of scope for an otherwise good performance to be ruined. It's a long race – a lot can go wrong. A marathon is an event that for most people, you can only attempt a few times per year at most. If something goes wrong, you may have a long wait until the next one. It's an important day – make sure practical aspects are in order.

Fifth, thinking through all the practicalities in advance might throw up questions that had not occurred to you. I always wrote down my schedule for the final few days before a race, with details of exactly what I would do and when. I used to do the same before major exams when I was younger. This process often brought up unforeseen questions that needed answering. Once I had a pre-race schedule which worked for me, I repeated it for each race with refinements and learning from my last marathon.

What are the practical details you need to organise and decide about for a marathon? The following are examples of decisions I made. It's a long list!

1. Accommodation: is it quiet, easy for travelling to the start, have everything you will need, and crucially, have the breakfast you will want on race day?
2. Travel to the start: how will you travel, at what time, how long will it take, will you reach the start in good time, do you have the right access passes, what will you do if the train/bus is full or delayed?
3. Food: for the final three days up to and including race-day breakfast, what will you eat, when, how much, is it suitable? The same applies to drinks.
4. Kit and shoes: what will you wear for any weathers, do you have spares of essential items, have you worn everything in, does it meet the competition rules, can you attach your race bib easily? What goes in your kit bag for afterwards?
5. After you finish: what will you do, where will you go, who will you meet and where, will you have food and drink available to help your recovery, enough warm clothes to put on, how will you travel home given road closures?
6. Warm-up: how much, when, what will it consist of, how long before the start will you finish it?
7. Race-day nutrition: how much will you drink, at what points in the race, have you practised this in training?
8. After race day: what will you do to recover as quickly as possible, how much rest will you take, how will you avoid catching infections?

You will have gathered from this that I am a details person, often excessively so. But organising all these details early meant that on race day, all I had to think about was executing my race plan. It made the prospect of racing a marathon feel diminished, and a less daunting task. It certainly made me feel eager, confident and on top of my game. I even looked forward to racing.

I have seen athletes, even at elite level, who have cut corners on practicalities. For example, not bothering with a recce of the course, not thinking ahead about race-day nutrition and making no preparation for predictably hot weather. In April 2004 while preparing for my first marathon, I did not think beyond the finish line. On race day, I struggled to walk after the finish and, because of poor planning, my journey home was much longer and more difficult than necessary. I recovered slowly, developed knee pain and was unable to run for several weeks afterwards. From my next marathon onwards, I always planned ahead how I would travel home.

Being well organised may seem obvious. But how you prepare the practicalities can have a major impact, both positively and negatively on your performance.

> **Always think through the practical details of race day, or a major event, in good time. It may seem onerous, but it is effort well spent. Hard work ahead of time will not go to waste.**

Now it gets tough!

Insight 26
Don't Be Dazzled

While watching the 2004 Athens Olympic Marathon, I remember being transfixed as Japan's tiny Mizuki Noguchi powered up the hills in the second half, destroying the rest of the field. She hung on to her lead to win in the ancient Panathenaic stadium. I was awestruck by her performance, but her humility and the absence of any flamboyant celebrations after the finish made me think Noguchi must be someone who simply works extremely hard. More than adoration or amazement, limitless respect was what I remember feeling after watching her win.

Between 2006 and 2011 while we lived in Tokyo, I met, observed and raced against Noguchi several times. In Sugadaira in Nagano Prefecture and in St. Moritz in Switzerland, during training camps when we happened to be in the same place at the same time, I was able to see a little of how she trained. Apart from members of the Tenmaya Corporate Team, I have never seen anyone train harder. I heard that she could squat twice her body weight, which for a marathon specialist is exceptional. Being so tiny but as strong as an ox, she flew up hills in the latter stages of marathons, when others struggled. In the 2007 Tokyo International Women's Marathon, she surged up the final long hill like she had in Athens, leaving others in the dust. Yet whenever I spoke with her, she was humble and understated, asking me how I was and generally being an ordinary person. There was nothing flashy or arrogant. I also sometimes had massage treatment from the same therapist who treated her. Most of these sessions involved me coping with the pain and occasionally sweating profusely. But I gathered that Noguchi often slept through her massage sessions; the pain obviously was not a big deal for her. It was such a privilege to be able to observe and learn from her. The only conclusion I drew from this experience was that there was no secret recipe; she simply applied herself diligently and trained hard.

In April 2012 we spent a month training at altitude in Mammoth Lakes, California. While there, I sometimes joined training sessions with Terrence Mahon's group including Deena Kastor, the 2004 Athens Olympics bronze medallist. This was a similar experience to what I had observed with Noguchi. All the athletes in Mammoth trained hard and looked after themselves. Again, there was nothing flashy, only consistent, steady hard work.

If an athlete is performing well, everyone wants to know how and why they are so good – what sort of training, how much speedwork and what they are eating. We all want to know how they have achieved success and what secret weapons they have up their sleeves. It is easy to jump to the conclusion that such a person must be doing something out of the ordinary, very special, or different from the rest of us. The media hype around success also lifts these people up onto pedestals – they seem to be superhuman, or living in a parallel universe, or possessing abilities that others can only dream of. All of this often makes us believe that we can't be like them.

Yet, time and again when I have observed clean world-class athletes, I have come to the same conclusion that they are only human, but are working exceptionally hard at their craft. There genuinely is no secret recipe, no special magic that is not available to the rest of us. It is worth remembering this because the dazzling effect of successful people means we sometimes give ourselves excuses not to try to be like them.

These experiences reinforced for me the importance of focusing your efforts on the basics and what matters, namely training, rest and fuel. All of these world-class athletes were doing this, at a very high level. None was skimping on these fundamentals. Equally, none of them – at least from what I saw – was too preoccupied with the additional extras which might gain you a few seconds here and there. Perhaps they were doing all they could on these extras and I simply did not see it. But without doubt, the overwhelming focus of their attention and physical effort was on the fundamentals.

One factor which contributes to the dazzling effect of success is sports science. In recent years this has become a huge and high-profile industry. We often read about the brilliant scientists behind the world's best athletes and all the magic they work in their charges. This reinforces the notion that ordinary folk can't be successful like the stars: unless you have scientific backing, and the money to afford it, you will not make it. There seems to be a perceived, widespread need to have all sorts of complicated kit and scientific input to make progress.

I think it's unfortunate if the role of science in sport makes would-be athletes believe that complicated science is essential to their progress. It's not. Further, in my experience, scientific input is only useful as long as you successfully make the link between scientific data and what you do as an athlete. Scientific data, in and of itself, is of limited use. It is what you do with it, how you interpret it, and how you use it in your training, which may be useful. It's no good being told to train at x intensity if your sleep is not good enough to recover and enable you to train at x.

Therefore, never let other people's success, and science's role in it, dazzle you into thinking that you can't also be successful. The fundamentals of success are train, refuel, recover and adapt. Scientific input into athletes' training has its value; but you can achieve an awful lot with simple hard work. Whenever you forget this, take a trip down memory lane to the great British male marathon runners of the 1980s. They ran world-class times, won medals and major races and broke records through sheer hard work while holding down busy full-time jobs. None of the science, gadgets and specialist equipment that is ubiquitous in running now existed back then.

> **Never allow the hype and aura around successful people stop you from thinking you can achieve your goals. Diligent, hard work is the answer. There is no secret recipe.**

Part Six
Review and Reflect to Improve

Insight 27
Stop, Rest, Think

After the Beijing Olympics, I remember taking only one week off running before resuming training. This short rest was despite the fact that my Olympic performance was the end point of four years of hard work. Finishing outside the medals left me with a feeling that if I had only given a little more, I could have been up there with the best in the world. This motivated me to return quickly and train harder.

I raced the Tokyo International Women's Marathon in November, only three months after the Olympics. Because I had lost too much weight, I lost a lot of strength. The following April in London I finally broke 2:25, running my final personal best of 2:23:12. Naturally, this progress was terrific. But thereafter, life became steadily tougher – a succession of injuries, frustrating performances and eventually retirement. If I had not been so impatient after Beijing and taken time properly to pause, rest fully and reflect, perhaps the years after that would have been easier. It's interesting that some athletes have very long careers, even spanning decades, but that includes fallow years because of injury, time out for having children, or other reasons. Perhaps these periods of enforced rest and time away from running allow for regeneration and a regime which is more sustainable in the long term. Because I was a relative latecomer to elite marathon racing and because it was our living for several years, I felt compelled to race frequently. I did not really feel the need for proper time away to rest before it was too late.

When you have completed a marathon or other major event, it's vital to take a little rest and a break. In my experience, this serves two main functions: making a full recovery; and using reflection on your recent performance to improve.

First, you need to rest your mind and body. Marathon racing is tough, no question. It takes a huge amount of physical and mental effort, from which you need to fully recover. On top of running the marathon distance, the nervous excitement of the day and everything that goes into it – travel, staying away from home, meeting friends and more – can be exhausting. You also must recover from all the training and preparation that you have put into it over several months, or even years. During this time, there may have been easier days or even weeks, but you never fully switch off from preparing for a marathon until it is over. The race ahead of you is always there so there is always something you could be doing to prepare for it. Maintaining this level of focus and effort all the time is impossible. You can't be on top form at all times. You need to allow for peaks and troughs in your ability to devote energy to a task. Therefore, there has to be time for proper, thorough rest after a marathon. What form that takes varies from person to person. It could be a holiday, a break from training, or an extended period away from running altogether. For me, mental rest was as essential as physical rest. Escaping altogether from running and having a proper mental break was critical for me to maintain motivation and enthusiasm for training.

The need for rest applies, regardless of how stellar your performance was. A positive race experience can leave you eager to get back and improve further. But equally, a poor performance can make you determined and fired up to return and do better next time. Enthusiasm to return is always welcome, but it can only come after sufficient rest. In the endurance running world, there are races available all year round. Unlike in other sports, there is no defined race season that allows for, and even forces you to take, time away from racing for proper rest during the off-season. It's even more important in the endurance world to take time off.

Some athletes seem to need little rest after major races. They can churn out world-class performances frequently, and have an enviable and incredible ability to recover quickly. But most runners are not like this and will need more rest.

Second, the time after a major race or event is crucial for review, reflection, and learning. It's a good opportunity to look back and engage in some honest self-assessment and clear thinking about what you did well and what needs to improve. This is best done while the race is still fresh in your memory. When reviewing a race, it is easy to focus on what did not go well that you would like to improve for next time. It's more difficult to give yourself credit for what you did well, but this really matters. Preparing for and completing a marathon is a huge task. It is worth appreciating at the time all the effort and hard work that went into it, not only from yourself but from people who have helped and supported you along the way.

After any major race, I wrote down a list of what went well and what did not. It could include anything and everything – split times, pace judgement, decisions

I took in the race, how I spent the days before the race, how I felt mentally and why, how I dealt with bad patches, practical aspects and interactions with other athletes. I like things to be organised so lists work for me, but perhaps a better tool for this is what I call brain-dumps – writing down everything that comes to mind in no particular order, even if it might seem tangential to your performance. Often these random thoughts can trigger further, related thoughts which are useful and warrant more careful consideration in slower time. By writing these reflections down, you can sometimes uncover elephants in the room – areas that you had previously not considered which may be having a major impact on your performance.

I was always competitive, wanting to improve and quite hard on myself. As a result, I often did not take enough time off after major races. This didn't matter in the short term, but eventually it caught up with me and the result was persistent injuries and having to retire.

> **After a major event, always take time to rest and reflect. This will lead to improvement and sustainable effort over the long term. Impatience to return too quickly can be costly.**

Insight 28
A Pat on the Back

Runners can be impatient for progress, always wanting to improve and reluctant to be satisfied with themselves. It's in the nature of the beast – running fast is exhilarating and satisfying, so it's natural to want to do it. Running, unlike some other sports, is very clearly measured. It is absolutely crystal clear who is fast and who less so. It's therefore easy for others to judge you by the times that you run over certain distances.

However, gaining recognition from others when you deserve it is a hit-or-miss business. Sport is famous for having armies of armchair critics who freely criticise athletes, even when they themselves are unable to do anything near as accomplished as the athletes they are judging. Therefore, being able to judge objectively and recognise your own efforts is a valuable skill to learn. You need to be able to give yourself credit when it is due. If you're dependent on praise from others, for example a coach, parent or teammate, for feeling good about yourself and your running, you are at the mercy of others who may have little understanding of you. Praise and encouragement when you deserve it may flow freely, but they also may not. It is a precarious place to be.

Especially for young athletes, developing the ability to assess yourself objectively and give yourself credit when appropriate is so important. To be able to recognise when you have performed well, you have to learn how to assess yourself honestly and decide what was good and what was not. Until you are the single best athlete in the world, there will always be rivals who are better than you. At every stage of your career, in terms of actual age, training age, and physical development, being able to judge where you are at is vital.

The aftermath of the 2008 Beijing Olympics was a mixed bag in terms of assessment of my performance. My goal from the start had been simply to make the team and race in the Olympics. This was enough; I had never set myself a goal in terms of time or place. Therefore, finishing sixth was way above my goal. I should have been over the moon and in some ways I was. To think that I was the sixth best marathon runner in the world was very satisfying.

However, several factors made me doubt myself. I was agonisingly close to the medals – 22 seconds after nearly two and a half hours of running. So near and yet so far. The winner was crossing the finish line as I was running around the track inside the Bird's Nest stadium. I wished I had run more aggressively but my experience at the previous summer's World Championships had knocked my confidence. The first comment my father made to me was, "But why didn't you run faster?" I left Beijing with a strange mixture of feelings. The sense that others viewed it as an underwhelming performance left me feeling disappointed, even though I genuinely thought sixth place was a result I could be proud of. In a nutshell, I was too influenced by what others said and did, which left me doubting my own belief that it was a good performance. I wish I had had more confidence in my own views. If I had, I believe I would have taken more rest and perhaps had fewer injuries in the years that followed.

At the London 2012 Olympics, I saw an example of this after Jo Pavey finished seventh in the 10,000m in 30:53:20. Jo was the first non-East African-born finisher. Her position and time were outstanding and truly world-class. Yet on return to the Team GB camp, she was apparently met with comments such as, "Never mind, better luck next time". Athletics is perhaps the most accessible sport in the world, which gives it unrivalled depth. The quality of competition is consistently and absurdly high. This, combined with the medals-at-any-cost approach of British sport in recent years, means that truly exceptional, world-class performances like Jo's may be viewed with disappointment. Thankfully, Jo appears to have the ability to judge her own superlative performances for what they are. Somebody with less conviction might have suffered more from this experience.

How can you develop the ability to objectively judge yourself and your performances? Setting clear, realistic goals is a good place to start, and then resisting the temptation to move the goal posts. Using objective, rather than subjective, measures is also useful. For example, using your time and finishing position rather than reactions from others. Remembering all the hard work that went into a performance beforehand, rather than thinking only about how you ran on race day, will give a fuller picture of your total effort. Identifying areas where you genuinely could have performed better, and thinking about how you might do this next time, will lead to positive learning for the future. Overall, this process is about focusing as much as possible on objective facts and relying less on subjective opinions.

My advice to runners at all levels is to take the previous insight and this one together and ensure that after every major race you take time to stop, reflect and review, and give yourself credit when it is due. Others may give you recognition, but don't count on it. If you write down your reflections, they will provide a trove of wisdom in future years when you can look back and seek inspiration from your past hard work. Occasionally, when I look back at my training diaries from the years when I was an elite athlete, I am amazed by them. I wonder if I really did what is in them. *Was the person who did this really the same person I am now?* It's inspiring to read now what my former self did, even if at the time I rarely felt it was good enough.

> Learn to judge your performances for yourself, honestly and objectively. When you perform well, give yourself credit, regardless of your environment or other people's judgements.

Insight 29
Celebrate!

When you have success, stop and savour it, appreciate it, and enjoy the moment. Improvement makes you feel terrific – there is nothing quite like running a personal best to make you feel invincible! It fires you up and makes you wonder how much more you have in you. It's easy to allow this excitement to push you on straight away to seek further progress. But before you know it, the moment to savour success will have passed, forever. Times like this are incredibly special, so when they happen take time to enjoy your success.

There were times as a full-time athlete when, although I was improving, I was impatient to improve more rapidly. I should have stuck with my existing routine which was delivering improvements and good results. But I was too greedy for bigger and better results and I changed what I was doing in pursuit of faster progress. This led not to improvement, but instead to me becoming overwhelmed with too much to do, overtraining and performance stagnating. Now that I look back, I wish I had been more patient and had the insight and maturity to see that what I was doing was right. I could have paused for longer after each race and enjoyed and appreciated any successes fully. Instead, I constantly ploughed on, eager to improve further.

Everyone's upward curve has to stop somewhere. None of us can continually become faster. At some point, we all stop improving but we never know when that will be. Elite sport is full of examples of athletes who have had their best performance but cannot see it. They continue striving to be better but end up struggling before retiring. It's difficult to see this when you are in the thick of competing; it's almost impossible to stand back and see the peak of a career when it happens. Therefore, it is vital to value good performances and be grateful for them when they happen but also to think carefully before you change something that is delivering for you. Success is fleeting and short-lived. If you are fortunate enough for it to come your way, make the most of it.

How one person defines success is, inevitably entirely different from someone else's definition. In distance running, an athlete's pedigree is transparently clear in hours, minutes and seconds. But at the end of the day, we are all human regardless of how fast we are. We all need to take time to enjoy any successes, no matter how we might each define them. Whatever success means for you, celebrate it when you achieve it.

If I look back at my races, the difference in how I felt afterwards relative to the actual performance is stark. In London in April 2005 in my second marathon, I finished tenth in 2:31:52. My previous personal best was 2:39:16. I qualified by eight seconds for the GB team for the Helsinki World Championships. I was absolutely elated with my performance. I thought 2:31 was an awesome time and spent several weeks afterwards savouring it. Yet in November 2008, I ran 2:25:03 at the Tokyo International Women's Marathon and was decidedly underwhelmed. It was still a personal best, by only seven seconds and I had moved from fourth to third in the final kilometres. But I was disappointed by what I saw as a lacklustre performance and not winning. The contrast with how I felt in April 2005 could not have been greater, even though I ran much faster and made the podium. I had upgraded my expectations of myself so drastically in the intervening years and was disappointed by a world-class performance. With hindsight, this now seems absurd. Why could I not find satisfaction in running 2:25? Having already run 2:25 three times and finished sixth in the Olympics, I felt enormous pressure to deliver world-class, exceptional performances at every outing. The result was losing the ability to savour and appreciate success if it was not quite up to expectations.

The importance of being thankful for success when it comes really hit me when I retired from elite competition. Suddenly I understood that much of the appeal of running to me was the regular fix of elation, satisfaction and sheer exhilaration which comes with a good performance or training session. Worryingly, I could also see that this source of self-worth was over. I would never run another personal best, never line up on an elite start again, never win another big race. This stark fact was a really unwelcome blow. I spent a long time in denial, unable to accept it. Running only became hard work and unsatisfying. It's clear to me now that the fix that running gives you could be like a drug addiction. I have never been addicted to drugs – except for caffeine and sugar! Therefore, I can't claim to know what serious addiction is like. But the precipitous collapse in how I felt day-to-day made it obvious that running had been giving my brain a daily boost that had kept me on an even keel.

I have now understood how precarious, dangerous even, this state of affairs is. You can't rely on racing marathons at world-class level to feel all right. It is no surprise that many elite athletes find themselves plummeting into mental ill-health when they retire. The regimented routine and regular fix of achieving something special are finished. Now I have radically readjusted what I define as success and drastically recalibrated what I strive to do each day. Doing three small, kind actions for someone else every day, running four or five times per week, and eating five-a-day, have become goals that I can aim for and work at. The coaching I do now is almost entirely for recreational runners. The excitement and satisfaction that progress gives them is so terrific to see. It's a much healthier way of life than being an elite athlete. Helping these runners, even in a small way to feel the satisfaction of making progress, is immensely rewarding.

Retiring from elite competition and the years that followed were a lonely, dark and frightening experience that I never want to repeat. The single biggest source of support that helped me through it was the Dame Kelly Holmes Trust. Being able to talk to other former athletes who had struggled after retirement and had empathy and understanding of my experience was such a blessing. Dame Kelly Holmes' vision in creating this charity, which also helps young people in difficult circumstances as well as former athletes, is exceptional. Her service to others cannot be overstated. The difficulties many athletes face after retiring highlight the value of stopping and savouring any moments of success – before it is too late.

Achieving success in anything is fleeting. Always appreciate it at the time. However you define success, celebrate it. You never know when it will come again.

Insight 30
Be Your Whole Self

Progressing in distance running requires the optimisation of a number of factors. It's not only down to the quality and quantity of training, though of course these are central. Rest, recovery, sleep, nutrition, hydration, injury-management and mental strength – the usual suspects – also play a central role. It's akin to keeping plates spinning in the air – you have to work at all of them, frequently. If you neglect any one factor for long enough, it will crash to the floor and ruin your hard work in other areas. Putting all your effort into one area, while slacking in others, will bring you progress of sorts, but only up to a point. Your hard work may not fully pay dividends if the other factors are neglected. Iron deficiency is a good example. Iron is needed for making new red blood cells and is critical for transporting oxygen round the body. If you are low in iron, your training may effectively be wasted because your body has insufficient iron to use when adapting to the stimulus of training.

Therefore, it is essential to see yourself holistically – to look at your entire routine in the round. It is important to assess objectively what may be preventing further improvement and take steps to rectify it. If you're not good at seeing yourself holistically, enlist the help of someone who is. A coach is an obvious example, but if they only see you at training sessions, they may have little knowledge of your eating habits, how well you sleep, and other relevant details. A family member or friend might be a better choice. Actually, a non-runner might be a good person for this task because they may be able to take a wider view than a fellow runner who is immersed in all the details.

I described previously how in 2005, I made big improvements in my lifestyle away from running. Until then, I had been too focused on training and had been neglecting all the additional factors that support quality training. I am a details person and was unable to see that by slacking on non-training elements, I was inhibiting more substantial progress. Once I had understood this and drastically improved my lifestyle, I made much faster progress. Coaches can encourage this process by asking the right questions of athletes about their lifestyle away from training, such as: Are you sleeping well? Are you eating a balanced, varied diet? How is work/studying going? Do you feel your work/life balance is about right? There may be a limit to how much interest a coach can take in an athlete's personal life. But they can encourage athletes to think about all the non-training elements and see if there is room for any of them to be improved.

Examples of factors that may inhibit faster improvement that I have come across include: athletes not eating enough; training routines lacking quality sessions; running loads exceeding what a runner's strength and robustness can tolerate; returning to training too quickly after a marathon without enough rest; drinking too much; ignoring common biomechanical problems such as glute dysfunction and tight hip flexors; and poor sleep hygiene. Work-related factors are often a major culprit too, for example: too much long-haul travel causing jetlag and disrupted sleep; too long spent sitting down in front of computers leading to poor glute activation and hip stiffness; and excessive stress preventing runners from training as planned. I often have conversations with runners about how these problems could be mitigated, as much as we discuss their training menu. I feel that improving a runner's work life, since work takes up so much time, can be the best way to help them improve. In all cases, if the athlete can see themselves in the round, with help from others if necessary, they can fix the impediment that is holding them back and make much better progress.

In the latter years of my career, I was not resting sufficiently between training sessions and was not recovering properly. I felt exhausted most of the time, was losing the thrill and excitement of training, ran disappointing races, and generally fell out of love with running. The cycle of supercompensation was no longer working because there wasn't enough adaptation between training. It wasn't all bad – sometimes I raced well and felt good, but these occasions were few and far between. I remember waking up on marathon race days and feeling weighed down by what lay ahead, not excited and eager to go to the start as I had in earlier years.

Now with the benefit of hindsight, it seems so obvious that I was not getting enough rest. I was approaching 40 and should have taken heed much more of how I felt. But training less and resting more is a difficult concept for ambitious athletes to accept. Naturally, you want to train more because it seems logical that it will make you run faster. How I wish now that I was better able to see myself holistically and make the decision to train less. I guess all runners over the age of about 40, whether recreational or elite, have to face this decision at some point. If you can stand back, see the big picture and bring wisdom and common sense to your decisions, you will end up with fewer, if any, plates crashing to the floor.

None of this is complicated. Much of it may seem obvious. But I think it's easy for us runners to get too drawn into the details of training day to day and the next race and miss or ignore something that might be important. In Insight 27, I explained the importance of stopping to reflect after a big race. This is the ideal opportunity while resting, to look at yourself from a distance and really think what might be holding you back from better performance.

> It's easy to lose sight of the bigger picture. Now and again, stand back, assess your routine in the round and check that all you are doing is serving a useful purpose.

Time to dig in!

Insight 31
Good Times Are Fleeting

Welsh marathon legend and former world record-holder Steve Jones's famous hamstring remark (Insight 13) is an acknowledgement that injuries can finish a runner's career in an instant. His pithy phrase captures perfectly how fleeting an athletics career can be. Running is an unforgiving sport; the wear and tear on joints and soft tissues is considerable, despite it being such a natural movement that humans evolved to do in the very distant past. Injuries are an integral part of distance running and can put an end to running quickly. Even if they do not end running altogether, injuries often curtail running and force you to run at a lower level.

Therefore, it is vital to enjoy every moment, every training session, every run out in nature, every race ... because you simply do not know when it will end. When you're training well, it can often feel like hard work, until you have to stop running because of injury – then you long to be back running again. It's easy to view races as the primary purpose of running and everything else you do is to that end. But racing is such a small part of the total time we spend running that it's a pity if training is viewed solely as a means to an end rather than an end in itself. Stopping now and again to reflect and take a wider view can help us to understand if, overall, our running is progressing as we want it to. If you become too stuck in the detail of daily training, good times can pass you by without you even noticing them.

Before the London 2012 Olympics, we joined the UK Athletics preparation training camp in Portugal. I had injured my foot in January, but it had settled down and almost cleared up entirely by May. I was able to race again in June and was looking forward to the home Games. But in late June it flared up again and by the time we went to Portugal I was having to work hard to manage it while continuing to train. With the Olympics imminent, it was very stressful to say the least! The stress clearly showed and one day Charles van Commenée took me to one side and told me to enjoy the journey, not only the destination. He was completely right – you have to enjoy every day, every step, every building block along the way, not only the competition that comes at the end. I was grateful to him for saying this so clearly, even though it was difficult to do what he was asking while dealing with an injury.

When everything is going well, and you're training consistently and running fast in races, it can feel like such times will go on forever. There may not be anything that gives you a sense of urgency. Average life expectancy nowadays is high and when you're young, a lifetime can look like an eternity stretching out in front of you. There were years and years when I felt like that. In 2009 I had finished second in London and was ranked second in the world. I felt on top of the world. But the start of the end of my career was already underway, even though I didn't realise it. Two diametrically opposed phases of my running were happening at the same time. As more and more time passed and I was struggling with injuries and frustrating performances, I began to realise what I had lost. I had hope that I might yet have my best performances ahead of me, but reality was steadily making that hope fade away.

Now looking back, how I wish somebody had said to me: "This will not last forever, you only have a few years, make the most of it while it lasts." I was so involved in the everyday details of training and racing that I was unable to see this for myself. Lifting myself out of the detail to see the bigger picture is definitely a skill which is still a work in progress. In any case, if any young athletes are reading this, I hope they will take my advice and make the best of every moment, now that they know their best years will fly by and eventually come to an end.

In practice, what can runners do to grasp every opportunity? If I had my time again, it would be this: whenever I am in two minds about doing a certain race or training session, I would always set my default option in favour of doing the race or session. This does not necessarily mean I would, in the end, do them all. There may be good reasons for skipping some. But erring on the side of doing them means you will talk yourself out of potentially special occasions less frequently. One regret I have with hindsight, is never having raced the European Championships Marathon. At the time, I convinced myself that there were good reasons to focus on other races. But opportunities like championships are rare; they deserve to be grasped with both hands.

My father was an avid runner and completed many marathons. He continued running into his seventies, doing what he could and mixing it up with walking. The last decade of his life was horrendously blighted by Lewy Body Dementia and

Parkinson's disease. Ironically, it was his love of running that made it clear that he was seriously ill. While out running one day, he found himself unable to run in a straight line and kept veering off involuntarily to one side. Very sadly, running for him was effectively over from that point. He tried to continue but couldn't run safely, frequently losing his balance and falling. In a cruel irony, being no longer able to do what he loved – running – was the signal that his life was starting to close.

We do not know what is around the corner. Embrace what you are able to do while you can. Careers in running, or indeed anything, can be over quickly.

Part Seven
Look After Yourself

Insight 32
Food Is Fuel

Food is the fundamental bedrock of all our lives. It is the fuel that gives us energy to be active and the source of protein, fats, carbohydrates and micronutrients that keep us healthy. These are all basic facts.

However, our eating habits are frequently hijacked by clever advertising, manufacturers whose primary objective is making money, food fashion, persuasive experts promoting particular foods, social expectations and customs and social media. Any of these factors can leave you eating sub-optimal nutrition that will affect your general health and certainly your running.

I am neither trained nor qualified as a nutritionist or dietician. What I learnt about nutrition came from two main sources: the need as an elite athlete to optimise my nutrition, so I sought out and gathered useful information as much as I could; and what I learnt from living in Japan, which has the highest life expectancy in the world and low levels of obesity.

The lessons I learnt and have used about nutrition are the following.

Variety is required: eating as wide a variety of foods as possible is the best way to obtain a range of micronutrients. It's easy to fall into eating habits that restrict the range of foods we eat. For example, having the same menu for breakfast or lunch every day. Or having a limited number of foodstuffs in any one meal, for example pork, rice and two vegetables – a total of only four foodstuffs. Or only eating foods which you like and being reluctant to try new foods. I always tried to eat a wide variety of foods. Whether it was enough or not, I don't know. But this was always the goal. I drew up a long list of foods, divided up into major food groups and ticked them off each day as I ate them. Therefore, I saw what foods I had not eaten in a while, or if I was eating one particular food too much.

Maximise highly nutritious foods: we often hear about these special foods, such as leafy green vegetables, colourful vegetables, oily fish, seaweed, shellfish and fermented foods. This is for good reason – they are better for us, in various ways, than other foods. As with variety, I always tried to maximise intake from these food groups.

Supplements: I took a small number of supplements when I was training hard, including iron, magnesium and vitamin B12. This was mainly to avoid depletion and its effect on performance. I was constantly trying to keep my weight down and being careful about the amount I ate. This, combined with huge amounts of training, means you risk not obtaining enough essential micronutrients. However, I am not a fan of supplements. They are not strictly regulated and there is the risk of contamination with banned substances. It can be difficult to measure their impact, though a nutrient like iron can be measured using blood tests over time. Also, they are expensive. But most important of all, humans did not evolve eating supplements – we evolved eating real food which we hunted and gathered. Our bodies have arrived at the form in which we find ourselves today based on real food. Why give them anything else?

Avoid restrictive or excessive consumption: these days, restrictive diets are everywhere and are fashionable. The plethora of reasons given for not eating certain food groups is extraordinary. But all restrictive diets, whatever the rationale on which they may be based, are in direct conflict with the need for variety. It's not for me to question or doubt the validity of other people's restrictions. But over the last few years these diets seem to have become ubiquitous. Similarly, excessive consumption of some foods, often to replace restricted foods, also reduces the variety in any diet.

Fuel during races: I experimented with various energy drinks and gels. I found gels too sweet and sticky, so I always used drinks in marathons. I aimed to drink enough during the race to prevent dehydration at levels which diminish performance but not too much. Excess fluid is extra weight you have to carry. You can afford to be a little dehydrated at the end of a marathon – after all, the race is over by then.

In 2004, I changed and improved my diet significantly. I believe this is one of the pivotal factors that enabled me to train harder and improve in the following years. I ate many more highly nutritious foods, many of them Japanese, including seaweeds (mainly *hijiki, wakame, kombu* and *kaiso* salad), fermented foods (mainly *natto* and *miso*-based dishes), fish and shellfish (*niboshi, unagi,* various kinds of shellfish and oily fish), soy products (*tofu, miso, aburaage,* beans, soy milk, *ganmodoki, okara*) and a wide variety of colourful and leafy vegetables. We also started making fresh smoothies every morning, again with a variety of fruit and vegetables. I missed foods from back home in the UK when I lived in Japan and was travelling for training and racing. I always stocked up on fig rolls during trips back to the UK. The supermarket down the road from our apartment in Albuquerque, New Mexico had a foreign foods section. Next to the Chinese, Thai, Mexican and other exotic foods was a British aisle! Tea, Horlicks, custard creams, shortbread ... it was very nostalgic, but I can't say particularly healthy shopping there.

I'm not in any way claiming to have had a perfect diet when I was an elite athlete. I certainly have my vices – coffee and chocolate are at the top of my list! I remember eating a chocolate bar on leaving the Bird's Nest stadium after the 2008 Olympics. After many months of no chocolate, this was my special treat. I often used thoughts of eating chocolate cake to persevere through the final, hellish kilometres of a tough long run. I ground out the final stages, desperate to reach the end, promising myself the treat of a well-deserved, delicious cake afterwards. Nearly always though, once the long run was over, I decided that I didn't need said cake after all. However, being able to look forward to it and think about eating it while I was out there suffering on long runs was all I needed!

The chocolate bar was my number one treat after the Beijing Olympics. But I allowed myself another after the marathon was over. I had been working so hard to ensure I was at race weight, and once the race was finished, I could forget about this for a short while. One of my favourite Japanese dishes is *katsudon* – pork cutlets on rice with egg and a delicious sauce. Its only downside is the enormous number of calories in one portion. The indoor bike at my local gym in Tokyo counted burned calories as you cycled, based on actual foods. The first food to pop up on the screen after about five minutes of cycling was a sweet. Then an apple, nuts and on it went, with more and more calorific foods appearing on the screen as time went by. If you cycled your socks off for about two hours, eventually a *katsudon* appeared; that is how many calories it has. We had agreed to eat *katsudon* on the evening of the marathon. But the sheer stress of getting me to the start line in one piece took its toll on Shige once the race was over and he wasn't feeling well. I went to the restaurant by myself. Unlike the chocolate cake on long runs, I couldn't let this one go.

Despite all my efforts to eat properly, from time to time at competitions, I saw elite athletes eating the most extraordinary food. At the 2005 World Cross Country Championships, I saw a member of the Ethiopian team eat for her race-day breakfast an enormous plate of French fries and nothing else. At the same event, during dinner on the final evening after all the racing was over, the desert buffet items were brought out by the waiting staff and whipped away by the athletes in a matter of seconds. I have never seen food disappear so fast.

Food is so fundamental to our health. Always prioritise a varied, well-balanced, nutrient-rich diet.

Insight 33
Precious Sleep

Runners often ask me how I managed to sleep the night before a marathon because the nerves and anticipation of the race the following day can make it difficult to fall asleep. I took the view that I should expect to sleep poorly the night before a marathon – it's only natural that you might feel nervous so close to a race. Instead, I made a special effort to get good quality sleeps in the preceding two to three nights. If I was well rested by the night before a race, I was confident that I would feel okay on race day, regardless of how my sleep on the final night turned out. Conversely, this helped me to sleep better on the final night because I was confident that whatever happened I would feel good on race day.

Sleep is another absolutely fundamental part of keeping us alive and functioning normally. If you slack on it, your general health may suffer and your running certainly will suffer. Sleep is necessary for regeneration and repair, which is a crucial part of the supercompensation cycle I previously described. This won't work as well as it might, if sleep is compromised. None of this is complicated. But as with food, sleep gets hijacked by all sorts of things – entertainment, work demands, stimulants, screen-time, jetlag, anxiety, social customs and expectations. When we are pressed for time, sleep is often something we skip to make time for what is more urgent.

However, for runners sleep is one of the most important activities you ever do. There really is no room for skimping on it. If you are busy, it is better to reduce other activities and maintain your sleep. It's hard to overestimate how vital sleep is for runners.

When I was training hard, I took various practical steps to optimise my sleep. Despite this, I often had disrupted sleep – so it was by no means perfect. I conducted a sleep hygiene self-audit with the help of physiologist Dr. Charlie Pedlar and a sleep coach. The purpose of this was to examine and improve all the various factors that might be reducing my sleep quality. The following are examples of how I improved my sleep.

1. Bedroom environment: this is the most fundamental factor for sleep and comprises a number of areas.

    » **Temperature:** ensure your bedroom is the right temperature for quality sleep. In summer in Tokyo, this was only possible by using air conditioning, which can be dehydrating and noisy. If you're training or competing in hot conditions, adjusting the temperature for good sleep is vital.

    » **Noise:** I have never been able to sleep through loud noise as many other people can. When travelling and staying in hotels, I always request a quiet room away from public areas, lifts, main roads, music sources, etc. I always have a pair of earplugs with me, no matter what.

    » **Light:** if you're lucky enough to be able to sleep in broad daylight, you are very fortunate. I have never been able to, so I use light-blocking curtains at home and when travelling for races, I sometimes taped black bin bags over the windows. During the summer in Europe, dawn starts early. I remember having all my hotel windows covered with black bin bags for the 2005 Helsinki World Championships.

    » **Humidity:** hotels that have sealed rooms where the environment is controlled electronically can become unbearably dry and you often wake up gasping with thirst. Becoming dehydrated by dry air in your room is the last thing you need before a marathon. The way I tackled this was to fill the bath about two centimetres deep with water before going to bed. The evaporating water moistens the air overnight. A humidifier is even better, if available. The opposite – a very humid environment such as the Tokyo summers, are a whole new level of challenge for good sleep. I tried to dry out our bedroom using air conditioning before bedtime to at least make it easier to fall asleep. After experimenting with various steps, I decided in the end that the best way to cope with high humidity is acclimatisation. After two or three weeks in such an environment, I found I did acclimatise and, thankfully, it became easier to sleep well.

2. Pre-sleep activity: we often hear that looking at screens, watching television and drinking or eating stimulants, among other things, before bed are not conducive to good sleep. I found that hard training also fell into this category. When I ran a speed session in the evening, it took a long time afterwards to calm down and be ready for sleep. I often spent hours lying in bed awake unable to sleep. Racing marathons was the worst in this regard. I never slept a single minute during the night after a marathon. I often spent these nights digesting the results, reviewing how the day had gone and catching up on emails.

3. Switch off your mind: thoughts racing round your head is another common cause of being unable to fall asleep. Psychologist Sarah Cecil taught me several useful tips to help with this aspect, such as: write down a list of what you have done that day to help bring the day to a close; write down anything that is bothering you so you can return to it the following day to decide how to address it. To this list, I added noting down what I will do the following day, so I can go to sleep knowing I have not forgotten to do something important.

Jetlag is another spanner in the works for disrupting sleep. Many of my major marathons came after long flights from different time zones because I mostly trained at altitude beforehand. The solution to recovering from jetlag for me was fairly simple: going out into daylight for light exercise on arrival, staying up until at least 9 p.m. and doing everything possible – the list above – to have a good night's sleep. The only time this did not work was when I arrived in Tokyo at 9 a.m., which happened often. Staying up until bedtime from an early start was too long and occasionally I succumbed to daytime naps. Once I fell asleep in the early afternoon for a short nap and woke up the following morning.

> **It cannot be overstated how important sleep is. Take time to set yourself up for good sleep. Frequently audit your sleep habits to ensure they are fit for purpose.**

Insight 34
Be Kind to Yourself

Consistent, specific and good quality training is the foundation for improving at running. Without it your body won't receive the stimulus it needs to adapt and become stronger and faster. Even more fundamental is the myriad of lifestyle factors that together enable hard training. A healthy, sustainable and positive lifestyle sets you up to train hard, recover and improve over time. In a nutshell, what I am advocating is looking after yourself well and being self-compassionate.

This is paramount, not only in practical ways, such as having a nutritious diet and preventing injury, but mentally too. Runners are competitive, push themselves and relentlessly pursue new challenges, personal bests or nailing a certain training session. It can be a harsh mindset to live with. Self-compassion can be hard to come by but it's vital. Without it, mental ill-health, injury and disappointing performances aren't far around the corner.

What exactly do I mean by looking after yourself? The following examples are habits that I always aimed to stick to.

Now and again, give up on training if you feel terrible. We have all been there – you set off for a training session and simply feel exhausted, unmotivated and out of sorts. From then on, an internal battle ensues about whether you press on regardless, or cut your losses and quit, or perhaps train but attempt less. This is a skill that all runners need to learn over time – the ability to recognise when you are not in a fit state to train hard and to make sound decisions in these circumstances. It's a difficult call. You can't quit training too often, or you will lose consistency. But occasionally you have to bring a little self-compassion to your decisions and allow yourself to rest.

Avoid setting yourself unrealistic expectations. I was often guilty of this during my career. I expected way more of myself than I could realistically deliver and the result was frequent disappointment. This is such a pity – why feel unsatisfied with a performance only because it's good, rather than very good? It makes no sense – life is too short!

Keep on top of practicalities that can ruin your hard work. Replacing worn-out trainers, taking a drink with you to training in hot weather, arranging a blood test if you feel ropey for a long time, wearing compression socks if your calves are sore. These are small habits that can make a world of difference, but they take a little effort to organise and can be overlooked when you are fully focused on training hard.

Be realistic about burning the candle at both ends. If you want to train hard successfully, there has to be some give in the system in other areas of your life. It's difficult to train hard while holding down a demanding job, going out frequently and fulfilling caring responsibilities. Occasionally, this has to happen, but it's unrealistic to do it continuously in the long term.

Take it easy before big races. If you have a top priority race approaching, dial down what you must do on other fronts in the days and weeks before, if you can. For example, you could take a day off work, avoid overseas trips or long journeys and catch up on sleep in the days and weeks leading up to a big marathon.

If you're prone to certain injuries, always be diligent about prevention. I've had *plantar fasciitis* several times on both feet and now always use silicone heel cups in my shoes. If ever I feel it coming back, I use a night splint in bed for a few nights which tends to nip it in the bud. My right glute muscles often become dysfunctional, which leads to all sorts of trouble. I stay on top of strength exercises and glute activations immediately before running to keep them functioning at a good enough level to support the running I want to do.

Avoid habits that involve risk of injury or illness. When I was competing full-time, I frequently had foot injuries. Therefore, I avoided open-toed and very flat shoes because they increased the risk of injury – it simply made me nervous wearing them. When I have been outside, I always wash my hands as soon as I return home to avoid infections. I was and still am careful about food hygiene. Of all the infections you can catch, gastrointestinal infections always make me feel the most wasted and devoid of any strength and certainly unable to run.

Allow yourself treats if you want them, in moderation. If you love the odd glass of wine or piece of cake, the value and enjoyment of having one now and again seems to far outweigh the value of foregoing those small luxuries in the belief that going without will make you run faster. I have met a few runners who have given up alcohol completely for the sake of their running, but met others who argue that being able to have a few drinks is the main reason why they run! I guess it all depends on what you consider to be the more luxurious treat.

Give yourself a complete break from running if you feel it's necessary. My running career has been on-and-off all my life. I've had spells of more than one hundred miles per week, but also periods of no running at all, easy jogging when I feel like it and everything in between. A complete break from running can be exactly what you need sometimes. It allows you to return to it, when you're ready, feeling re-energised.

Plan plenty of fun, absorbing activities that are totally unrelated to running. Training can dominate your life – not only the time it takes, but also in terms of the need for rest afterwards and the activities you have to forego to do it. Let's be honest: running can make life quite mono-dimensional at times. Now and again, for the sake of having a well-rounded life, leave running behind and do something completely unrelated.

> **Look after yourself as best you can. Having balance and self-compassion in your everyday life is vital.**

Insight 35
Healthy Mind, Healthy Body

We all have ups and downs throughout our lives. Most of the time we deal with the downs by problem solving, resting and fixing whatever has gone wrong. We return to normal and life goes on. But if, for whatever reason, problems persist and you're unable to return to normal, it will be difficult to work at and achieve success in anything. This is similar to how depression starts. We all experience bad times and for most people these are short-lived. But if life is really tough and we can't escape from the bad times, feeling low all or most of the time can become the norm. Mental illness affects your physical health and doing everyday activities becomes exhausting, if you can do them at all. If you are struggling in your non-running life, whatever the cause, you have to be realistic about what you can aspire to and achieve in running.

The year 2011 was such an experience for me. Everything seemed to be going badly. I persevered as best I could, but my running was – unsurprisingly – lacklustre. With hindsight, I wish I had seen more clearly what was happening at the time and taken steps to make life a little easier, rather than continuously ploughing on regardless.

In January 2011 I stopped running to rehabilitate a chronic high hamstring tendinopathy injury. I didn't run at all between January and June. I missed the exhilaration and enjoyment of running outdoors and racing. Meanwhile, I was killing myself doing cross-training, trying to stay fit so that on return to running, I could qualify for and gain selection for the 2012 London Olympics. In between, I was spending several hours two or three times per week travelling across London to Lee Valley to receive treatment for my hamstring. Most evenings on returning home from Lee Valley I went straight to cross-training again.

In February 2011 we had moved back to London from Tokyo. Almost as soon as we arrived, the Tohoku earthquake happened and we watched in disbelief at the scenes of devastation on our television screens. We felt helpless being so far away and unable to do anything much to help from a distance. There was a strange sense of unease and guilt about having escaped from Japan so recently when the earthquake struck and seeing the extent of horrendous suffering going on there.

At about the same time, my father's health deteriorated rapidly because of progressing dementia and Parkinson's. At the time, these diseases were not diagnosed fully and were not being treated properly. Living alone, he was totally unable to look after himself but stubbornly refused to accept the help he needed, receive essential care or move into a care home. Often, he fell or another crisis blew up. I dropped everything, drove to Oxford and got him out of hospital, or dealt with the latest crisis. This situation was extremely stressful and draining.

By the end of 2011, finally something good happened and I managed to qualify and earn selection for the 2012 Olympic team. Almost to the day of being selected when, finally, I thought things were turning upwards again, I sustained a new injury, this time to my foot. That cleared up after a few weeks. In January 2012 I had another foot injury. Ironically, I sustained this injury doing dynamic drills to improve my finishing speed at the end of marathons, which had often cost me top places in the past. By the time this second foot injury happened, I had totally and utterly had it with s**t coming my way. It felt like a continuous stream of trouble was happening, with almost no good times in between; if there were any, they were fleeting and short-lived. If I didn't have the Olympics to look ahead to and get up for every morning, I think I would have given up altogether. I had reached and exceeded my limit of what I could stand and maintain any semblance of being in a normal state of physical and mental health. Although I managed to resolve the second foot injury and was in reasonable running shape as the Olympics approached, my performances in 2012 reflected how difficult things had been for a long time.

Naturally, none of this matters compared to the suffering that people all across the world endure every day from conflict, poverty and horrific abuse, to being the victims of crime and life-threatening diseases. First world problems and elite athlete problems perhaps count for little in the grand scheme of things.

But I think they are relevant, in terms of how they compare to your ability to cope with them. Even if the difficulties in your life pale in significance compared to those of others, if you don't have the skills to deal with them effectively, they may have a devastating impact on you and the people around you. If you're unable to tackle problems promptly and effectively and you find yourself struggling mentally and physically, running well will be hard. Running without pressure can be a very welcome escape and solace in such circumstances. As can spending time alone in nature, freeing yourself from whatever has sent you into difficult times. But running as a way to push yourself, achieve goals and break personal bests will only add pressure. It will not come easily.

If I could live through this period again, I would have taken a step back, accepted that I was not coping and decided that something had to give. I believe this would have led to a better outcome all round, rather than simply battling on regardless. Accepting your own limitations, and recognising when you have exceeded them, can be a much wiser and better way of dealing with difficulties than persevering no matter what.

> **If you are struggling, achieving any success will be difficult. Stand back, be honest with yourself and accept it when you cannot cope.**

Not long to go now!

Insight 36
Switch Off

Kumejima is a tiny island in Okinawa Prefecture, about 100 kilometres west of the main Okinawa Island in southern Japan. It is a semi-tropical paradise of white sandy beaches and stunning sunsets. During a quiet period of training, we visited Kumejima for a break. I was invited to run in the local half marathon as a guest so it was not entirely rest, but getting away was incredibly refreshing. Kumejima's main industry is growing sugarcane and the race took us through endless fields of tall sugarcane plants towering above us.

We discovered that the main attraction of this race was, perhaps more than the race itself, the after-party. Being so remote, visitors to the island are dependent on flights and there was a four-hour gap between most runners finishing the race and the next flight off the island. The organisers duly decided they had to fill this time with non-stop entertainment. It was the most epic after-party I have ever seen. Local *Okinawa awamori,* a very strong alcoholic drink, was flowing freely on demand, local dancers laid on flamboyant performances, every runner with a birthday was given cake and sung "Happy Birthday" to, every local dignitary gave a speech and on it went. It turned out that most of the participating runners were not first-timers but had been before. The famous after-party had brought them back year after year.

Like many races in small Japanese towns and villages miles from Tokyo and other big cities, the locals were bursting with pride about their home, the local food and other unique specialities of the area. They showed off all the local highlights to visitors with the warmest, kindest and most generous hospitality imaginable. This was a real highlight of living in Japan as an athlete – travelling all across Japan for training and races. Hagi, Matsue, Shizuoka, Matsuyama, Iga, Okayama, Himeji, Kobe, Kyoto, Hakuba, Nobeoka, Fujimi Kogen, Sapporo, Fukuoka, Sugadaira, Inuyama, Tokushima, Izumi, Marugame, Kumejima, Ishigaki, Ohme ... running took us to so many fascinating places that we may not otherwise have visited.

Being an elite athlete is not a nine-to-five job, it is a 24/7 job. You are your work. You may only train a few hours a day, but how you spend all the rest of your time can and will influence your performance. Resting, looking after yourself, receiving physical therapy of various kinds, sleeping, eating – your entire existence can affect your performance. There is no let-up. You can't switch off when you 'leave the office' as it were and let your hair down. This inability to escape entirely from your work means you must devise ways, as best you can, to get away from it and rest. Without this, you run the risk of becoming stale or losing your motivation and enthusiasm. This applies to mental energy as much as physical – delivering a maximum effort in races takes a huge amount of mental and nervous energy. It's difficult to do this if you have lost your enthusiasm for running. The same applies at non-elite level. Although recreational runners may not be training full-time, the need for rest, maintaining freshness and getting away from running sometimes still matter.

I found there is a big difference between simple rest – namely, sleep or lying down – and fun activities that are absorbing and transport you to another world. Both could be called time off, but their effects are dissimilar. The first is physically restful; it may be mentally restful too. Whereas the latter can be physically demanding but mentally are very refreshing and rejuvenating. Both have their place, but I found I needed to do the latter to feel properly refreshed and keen to run again. When you're exhausted from training though, sometimes crawling into bed is all you can manage. In the goals sheets I drew up, sports psychologist Sarah Cecil encouraged me to schedule 'fun' things on days off. This was to ensure that I did enough of those mentally refreshing activities. Spending time off only physically resting is welcome and necessary, but to really sustain hard training long term, you must truly get away from running from time to time and fully switch off.

I always took one day of complete rest during a cycle of training. This was one week early on, but I extended it to eight or nine days later, as I was not able to squeeze in all the training I needed to do and still recover. On these days off, I always tried to do something totally unrelated to running, to fully take my mind away from it and feel refreshed when I resumed training. Full-time marathon training is relentless and it helps if, through rest, you can maintain the drive to get out of the door and train hard every day. Many athletes are able to train every day for long periods without any days off. That is great if they can sustain their enthusiasm. But I found I really had to take days off to recover fully. I remember making short trips to Santa Fe, Taos and Flagstaff while we were staying in Albuquerque for altitude training. We visited the Georgia O'Keeffe museum on one trip, which was delightful. Being immersed in the world of an artist was the exact opposite of running and so refreshing.

The fallow period after major races is the best time for an extended break from running. While training for a marathon there was no time for much else. We always planned fun and exciting travel or other activities while enjoying a break after races. We visited Capri Island in southern Italy one year, a gorgeous oasis off the coast of Naples. This was early May and the island's flowers were at their best, while the weather was not too hot.

While trying to ensure I could genuinely switch off on days off, I never did anything that might end in injury, which mainly meant other sports, such as skiing or playing tennis. Call me boring, but I couldn't see the point of taking the risk of throwing away years of hard work because of one foolish decision. Accidents happen and when reading about the occasional career-ending injuries that athletes end up with, I decided it was safer to look after myself and ensure I could continue running, no matter what. If running had not been my living, I might have been more relaxed about risky activities, but it was our income so it was a simple choice to make.

Time off is vital for maintaining enthusiasm and motivation. Always make time for it.

Part Eight
Survive Hard Times

Insight 37
Hang in There!

Japanese marathon legend and two-time Olympic medallist Yuko Arimori once told me about an unfortunate incident before the 1992 Barcelona Olympics Marathon. The race was due to start in the evening at 6:30 p.m. During the morning on race day, she went to the bathroom in her hotel room to wash her face. Accidentally, she washed a contact lens out of her eye and wasn't able to retrieve it and put it back in. She did not have a spare with her. She panicked, wondering what to do. But she thought about what she really had to be able to see to race the marathon. The answer was the road and her drinks bottles. She realised that with only one contact lens, she would be able to see at least this much. In her mind, she switched her thinking from worrying about losing a contact lens, to believing that if she could see the road and her drinks, she would be fine. During the race she did not think about wearing only one contact lens. It simply did not affect her in a negative way. She maintained a high level of concentration throughout and won a medal. She could have lost her composure, or even withdrawn from the race. But instead, she pressed on, made the best of a bad situation and delivered a brilliant performance.

When things go badly for whatever reason, it's easy to lose your motivation, enthusiasm and willingness to work hard. Looking forward and aspiring to achieve a good outcome is what keeps us going much of the time, especially when we're taking on a tough challenge. But if you allow your thoughts to deteriorate, a bad situation becomes even worse. If you can, it's always better to commit to making the best of whatever scenario you find yourself in, however bad it may seem. You must cling to hope!

One strategy I use for persevering through difficult times is setting small goals. The most common scenario I used this for was the latter stages of a marathon. In the final kilometres, you're invariably suffering but the finish can be a long way away. I set myself small, quickly achievable and immediate goals to work towards. For example, as I mentioned in Insight 22, I focused on reaching the next lamppost, or the next mile marker, or hanging onto another athlete, no matter what. Towards the end of the 2009 London Marathon, when I was racing against Irina Mikitenko for the win, she kept throwing in surges and I stuck with her, come what may. Eventually, it was one surge too many and a small gap opened, allowing her to go on to win.

Once I had achieved a small goal, I created another one and another one. By doing this, time passes more quickly. By distracting your brain from how bad you feel, you maintain your performance better than if you fall into a spiral of negative thoughts. By setting myself small goals over and over, before I knew it the finish was within striking distance and I had survived the worst section of the race.

Reducing previously ambitious and lofty goals down to the bare minimum was another strategy I used, especially for periods of injury. When injury strikes, you're often forced to give up weeks, maybe months, of carefully laid plans and risk losing form that you have worked hard to build up. This is tough – I think you experience a grief of sorts for what you know you will lose. In these scenarios after a period of denial and anger, I always tried to reduce my goals to the bare minimum of what I could achieve, to ensure I had something positive and motivating toward which to direct my efforts. These might include: revisiting my sleep hygiene to ensure optimal recovery from injury; using process goals with my daily nutrition; starting each day by doing my best on my rehab programme; arranging to cross-train with a friend; and ensuring I had something fun planned that was mentally refreshing. If times were really bad I reduced my goals further to simply get out of bed at a respectable time, get dressed and have a good breakfast, before embarking on rehab or cross-training. This helped me to stay motivated and focused on the most important task at hand – recovering from injury – but also keeping a positive mindset while doing it.

Before the 2010 London Marathon we were staying in Albuquerque, New Mexico, for altitude training. Twelve days before the marathon we were due to fly to London. But a volcano in Iceland erupted and our flight, along with many others, was cancelled. There seemed to be a good chance that we wouldn't make it to London at all. But we decided to do our best to get there, however possible.

We embarked on a week-long odyssey of whatever journeys were possible strung together to eventually reach London. This involved flights from Denver to Newark and on to Lisbon, followed by a taxi ride to Madrid. Then, we drove a rental car to Paris because we couldn't find seats on any trains; took another taxi, this time to

Le Touquet on the French coast. From there we flew in a tiny plane to Shoreham-by-Sea, where a London Marathon driver picked us up for the final drive to London. We arrived in London on the Thursday evening before race day, having barely slept for a week. All I had eaten was what we could find in airport and local shops along the way. I had done little training – only the odd jog here and there when we had time. None of any of this journey was planned – we had to find whatever transport was available at each point. If you could imagine the worst possible way to spend the last twelve days' build-up to a marathon, this was it!

Race day arrived and I didn't have high hopes for my performance. I was stiff and mentally tired from our epic journey. I had spent all of the second half of 2009 recovering from *plantar fasciitis* and this was my first marathon in a year. Yet, I ran 2:26:16, a respectable time and not that far off 2:25 which, apart from running 2.23.12 in 2009, was the best time I had run most often up to that point. After all the stress and upheaval of the journey, in the end the result was not that bad. I had made the best of a bad situation and it turned out all right.

> **When things are going badly, simply do your best. A positive outcome is still possible and doing your best will make that more likely.**

Insight 38
Throw in the Towel

In some languages, there are words that do not have an exact equivalent in your own mother tongue, which for me is English. They capture beautifully a particular meaning or scenario that would take several sentences of explanation in other languages. It's much easier simply to use that untranslatable word with others who understand it, rather than embark on lengthy explanations of what you mean in your own language. I love this phenomenon − it's helpful and makes me feel fond of these words when I adopt them into my own language.

Japanese has a few such words and *gaman* is one of them. Dictionaries translate it as patience, endurance, tolerance, perseverance, self-denial and self-control. You could add to that list putting up with, hanging in there and getting by. As you can imagine, the word *gaman* crops up often in the marathon world. You have to *gaman* when training long distances, when trying to reach the finish in a race, and when making lifestyle sacrifices to help your running. Going without chocolate for many months before the Beijing Olympics required *gaman*, believe me!

This word goes to the very heart of Japanese culture. Japanese are patient, hard-working, willing to put up with stuff for the greater good, stoic and long-suffering. Being expected or told to *gaman* is completely normal; it is simply something everyone has to do at times. Living in Japan and trying to fit in there, I did my best to *gaman* when it was called for. In many ways this was a huge help for my running. Seeing others *gaman* without complaining or making a fuss made me do the same. It really helped me to make it through hard times, find the patience to get through hard long runs and exercise self-discipline, all of which are helpful for the marathon.

However, the longer I lived in Japan, the more I started to believe that *gaman* is only valuable up to a point. Eventually, diminishing returns set in. There is a strong sense around *gaman* that you do not question what you have to tolerate − you simply do it. But the trouble with this is you can end up with habits and practices that are not helping you to train and race well, nor to function well more generally. There is a tendency to overdo things because you think you have to *gaman* and you can lose sight of logical, fact-based rational decision making. If you have a tendency to train excessively anyway, as I do, feeling you have to *gaman*, no matter what can simply exacerbate this.

You must be able to *gaman* to be good at the marathon, no question. It's a long race, calls for huge amounts of training and you must have the mental patience and ability to tolerate suffering to run fast. I went through many tough times such as persistent and frequent injuries, and training hard alone. I used the spirit of *gaman* to get through them. But eventually you have to stand back and realise that tolerating hardship may simply be grinding you down. In these scenarios, changing course or quitting is sometimes better than pressing on regardless. You won't line up on the start line of a race feeling mentally raring to go if you are feeling constantly worn out. It is a fine balance to strike between being disciplined and working hard and listening to your mind and body when they are doing too much.

I doubted the value of *gaman* mostly when I was injured. Managing an injury can consume an inordinate amount of time and energy compared to when you are running injury-free. Fitting in cross-training, treatment of various kinds and rehab exercises can be draining and takes much more time than only running. My mental health often suffered during periods of injury. When you're injured, your drive to tolerate hardship often increases – you want to recover and get back out there. Any amount of *gaman* is worth it to be able to run again. But this can be unhelpful for recovery. Injuries happen for a reason, unless they are the result of a freak accident. Injuries are a clear indication that something has gone wrong. In times like this, more than anything your body needs rest and recuperation.

When I was recovering from *plantar fasciitis* in 2009 and from a hamstring tendinopathy in 2011, I remember my routine being relentless. I got up early to cross-train, travelled to have treatment and therapy, travelled home and trained again, and squeezed in strength and conditioning, massage, stretching, plus everything else you have to fit into a day in the evening, when I was worn out. I felt exhausted much of the time and there was little or no time off. At the time, I thought I was doing the right thing, squeezing in all these elements. But now I look back, I wish I had simply rested and slept more. If I had allowed my body to do its own recovery a bit more, I'm sure I would have returned sooner. Instead, I worked too hard, didn't get enough rest and my return to fitness and racing took many months. Rather than continuing to *gaman* relentlessly, I wish at times I had thrown in the towel and acknowledged that what I needed was more rest.

Japanese athletes' ability to *gaman* makes them world-beaters, if they have the resilience and energy to stand hard training. From what I know of how Mizuki Noguchi trained, it's no wonder at all that she crushed the field at the 2004 Athens Olympics. That race was probably a walk in the park compared to what she was used to every day. The uphill and downhill stages near Mt. Fuji of the Hakone Ekiden produce herculean feats of *gaman* that you rarely see in other events. The poor men's legs buckle under them, but they have to keep going because it's a relay. Equally, occasionally you see performances by Japanese athletes where they are clearly worn out by overtraining.

Perseverance is everything in the marathon – or any other major project. But only so far. At some point, you have to stand back and accept that you may need to change course.

Insight 39
When Something Breaks

Injuries are the bane of most runners' lives. I don't know of a single runner who has escaped injuries entirely. From wear and tear and overuse niggles to freak accidents and acute pain, injuries come in a range of guises and none of it is good! They cause trouble and misery wherever you look in the running world. But injuries can also galvanise us to work harder, make us appreciate it more when we are fit and injury-free, and fire us up to return even stronger. Seeing elite athletes perform brilliantly despite struggling with injuries certainly inspires. Perhaps it's not all bad after all!

Since injuries are part and parcel of distance running, it's worth investing a little time and energy in prevention. It will save you a lot of heartache, I promise! I've had a range of injuries over the years: *plantar fasciitis* and high hamstring tendinopathy that I mentioned earlier, plus *peroneal tendonitis*, an adductor tear, iliotibial band syndrome, sciatica, a heel bruise, pain between my toes, a bone stress response, a grumpy piriformis, hip trouble, ankle trouble ... as you might expect, it's a long list! Thankfully, my knees have held up beautifully and given me great service – so far.

The two key insights I learned from dealing with injuries are: prevention is always less stressful than cure; and use your common sense and simple remedies before diving into complex or expensive treatments.

On the first of these, prevention is self-evidently a good approach, but how? I always followed these simple steps.

1. Strength and conditioning: your body needs to be strong, robust and conditioned enough for you to be able to do the running you demand of it without breaking. A balance needs to be struck between strength and running load. Therefore, I always recommend some form of strength and conditioning for all runners of any ability. My tips on how to create a tailored programme for yourself are in Insight 5.

2. Increase training load gradually: volume, intensity and frequency all contribute to training load. Your body's tissues, such as muscle, bone, tendons and ligaments, all need time to adapt to any training stimulus. Increasing training gradually will enable adaptation without injury.

3. Work your glute muscles: glutes are a central, important muscle group which have various important jobs to do, such as hip extension and stabilisation as you plant your foot. Dysfunctional glutes seem to be very common, partly from all the sitting we do. If you have time for only one item of injury prevention, make it five minutes of glute activations immediately before running.

4. Be vigilant: many runners, myself included, seem to be prone to the same injuries cropping up repeatedly. This may be due to genetic factors, biomechanical problems or lifestyle habits. If you keep a close eye on these frequent injuries and what causes them, you can nip them in the bud before they become serious next time.

The second lesson I learned for dealing with injuries was using common sense and a simple approach. You may well need specialist treatment from a trained practitioner, but some injuries can be resolved simply, such as the following.

1. Footwear: changes in shoes are a common cause of injuries. If you imagine the number of foot strikes your body endures during training, it's easy to see how injuries can crop up if shoes cause your feet to function differently, even by a tiny amount. The width, cushioning and flexibility of shoes can all have an impact on how your foot works.

2. Rest: injuries happen for a reason and sometimes this will be overdoing things. Before diving straight into cross-training and a rehabilitation programme, ask yourself if a few restful days completely off training might be the answer.

3. Sudden changes: anything drastically new in your training routine can trigger injuries, such as training on different surfaces, gradients and terrain. The same applies to anything new in your non-running life. During COVID lockdowns, I've heard several runners complaining of excessive stiffness from working from home rather than commuting to an office.

4. Hot and cold: acute, local inflammation can easily be addressed with icing and rest. Increasing circulation to an injury can be achieved using hot and cold contrast baths. My history of tendon injuries tells me that tendons can be slow to heal; I often tried to speed this along with heat and cold.

5. Food for repair: our bodies need protein to regenerate. A new injury appearing may be a good opportunity to revisit whether or not you are eating enough protein from various sources.

Injuries are such a frustration for many runners. They break up your routine of training, which means losing not only training but being out in nature, seeing your friends and escaping from work. Taking care of your mental health during spells of injury can help to reduce the impact of this disruption. Arranging to see friends, doing other physical exercise and scheduling fun activities will all contribute to keeping a positive mindset while coping with injuries.

While altitude training in St. Moritz one summer, a bout of *plantar fasciitis* reappeared. I thought I had fully resolved it but unfortunately it lingered on. I had to reduce my running and focus instead on cross-training to maintain my fitness. My cross-training menu included uphill cycle rides from the nearby village, Samedan, for about 20km of cycling all the way up to the top of the Bernina Pass. I could really feel the increasing altitude as I rode. A distance of 20km is nothing much to serious cyclists but it was a tough and really enjoyable workout. After winding my way up the hairpin bends and winding road to the Pass, the view from the top was a nice reward!

> **Injuries are frustrating, no question. But there are plenty of positive and simple steps you can take to reduce their impact.**

Insight 40
Accept the Down Times

Most runners really love running – it's why we do it. The exhilaration of running fast and feeling fit, being outdoors in the fresh air, clearing your mind, training with your friends ... there is much to love about it. Running is physically hard, so there has to be some love there to make you do it. Running is the most natural of human movements. It's how we hunted and gathered and have survived all this time.

But sometimes running is not all a bed of roses. Injuries, chronic fatigue, feeling out of sorts, disappointing performances, lack of time for training, and any number of other reasons can cause you to fall out of love with running. Then what do you do? In my experience, recognising and accepting these down times is indispensable to finding a way to renew your love for running.

I have had an on-off relationship with running all my life. I did not run at all in an organised way during my childhood. As a teenager, I ran regularly but not at a high level. As a student, I ran more seriously and trained hard. While I was working full-time for the Foreign Office, I ran at a variety of levels – seriously while I was learning Japanese, but in a very ad hoc way when I was in demanding desk jobs. For several years I trained hard while working part-time and job-sharing at the Foreign Office. Then I became a full-time athlete and running was my life, all day, every day. After retiring and returning to the Foreign Office, I barely ran at all. Now that I am self-employed, I run about five times per week.

This mix of levels of running was caused by a variety of factors. Sometimes work was too demanding and a lack of time or energy stopped me from running more. At other times, I had the will to train hard but wasn't in a good training group and struggled to train hard alone. There were also times when mental and physical burnout made any serious running too hard.

There have been a few times when I've fallen out of love with running. My desire to do it simply disappeared. I either stopped or, if I had to continue, it became a chore and not at all enjoyable.

Chronic or frequent injuries have been a common cause. I have successfully overcome injuries numerous times. If it's one injury and relatively short-lived, it's not hard to hang in there and maintain hope. But repeated, chronic or long-lasting injuries are much tougher, both mentally and physically. Once you feel low, it's hard to find the cause of your sadness, namely running, appealing. Overdoing things has also made me fall out of love with running. Too much training, or too much high-pressure competition without sufficient rest in between, has led to what you might call burnout. But external factors have been prominent too. Doping and all that enables it has been a major external factor.

What to do if you fall out of love with running? If you have loved running at some point and physically can still do it, it's unfortunate if a bad patch means you leave running behind forever.

The answer, in my experience, is to adjust, change tack and find a way of running that can bring you enjoyment again. Asking yourself what it is exactly that you love, or previously loved about running can help with this process. For me, being out in nature is paramount. Running in green spaces is a way for me to bond with the natural environment. Seeing the seasons changing, wildlife, beautiful views and other wonders of nature is something I really miss when I can't run. It's difficult to describe, but when I'm stuck in an urban environment without easy access to parks, I find it mentally tough. Even if I don't actually go to a park very often, the fact of it being nearby and being able to get to easily if I want to is reassuring. Living near Yoyogi Park and later on the Tamagawa river in Tokyo were essential for me in such a densely populated and urbanised city. Both these oases of green space provided fresh air, nature and camaraderie with other runners that were very special.

Spending time with my friends is another reason why I love running. Putting the world to rights with a good friend while you pound out the miles is truly cathartic. During 2004-5, I often trained early in the morning before work with Lucy MacAlister in southwest London, sometimes along the river towpath in pitch darkness. Alongside training, we solved problems, dreamed of glory in upcoming races, caught up on gossip and generally set things straight for the days and weeks ahead. This routine was so special and I really missed it when I moved to Tokyo in January 2006.

If you are physically or mentally exhausted, complete rest and time away from running may be the answer. It's hard to decide how long a period of rest might be needed until you try it. Taking yourself totally away from running and immersing yourself in other hobbies or activities can work wonders by refreshing you and rekindling the urge to run.

Changing your running routine might be the answer. For anyone over the age of 40, often less is more. If you have been an active runner under age 40, the temptation is always to run more and more. But as we age, the risk of this leading to overtraining and injury increases. Now at age 48, I have accepted that I can't train anywhere near the level at which I used to train. I tried doing this for a few years and ended up exhausted and injured constantly. Now, I train at a much lower level and prioritise consistency before quality. Setting performance goals for training or races often makes things worse. Sometimes I leave my watch at home and simply run as I feel. Kilometre splits, pace and distance covered are sources of pressure that I can do without sometimes. If I feel really bad, I leave home when I had planned a run and I walk. After about ten minutes, I run for one minute and walk again. If that goes okay, I run again, this time for two minutes, then I build it up to three, four, five, and back down again. By doing this, I can exercise for one hour, of which 25-30 minutes will be running. Usually, I feel fine by about halfway and in good spirits by the end.

My core piece of advice if you find yourself not enjoying running anymore, is first to recognise that fact. Accept that something is not quite right. Feeling you should be loving running will not help. Think about what it is that you loved before. Tweak, adjust and adapt your running to include what you know you enjoy. If you really need to, simply take a break altogether. There is no shame in that.

Sometimes, running or whatever you love may lose its appeal. There will always be bad patches. Accept them, take a break, or adjust your habits. You may find that this renews your enthusiasm.

The finish is in sight!

Insight 41
Adapt and Move On

In running, as in the rest of our lives, there will always be factors which are unhelpful, frustrating or have a negative impact on you in some other way. Often these are things that we may not be able to fully control. They happen and there really is not much we can do about it. You can spend time feeling angry, complaining and seeking redress. But eventually, if you can't change the source of the trouble, you simply have to change your approach. On running, this could relate to anything – your training routine, shoes and kit, how events are organised, safety while out running, the people you train with, and how work affects your training.

How events are delivered can lead to a variety of frustrations for runners. Examples include: what drinks are provided during the race; where and how you leave your belongings before the race and retrieve them afterwards; start line procedures; marshalling; and sign-posts. None of these factors are likely to change, at least not quickly. But in the short term, adjusting your approach to deal as best you can with unhelpful logistics gives rise to less frustration and physical and mental energy wasted.

In October 2018, I ran in a trail race on Exmoor. My race was supposed to be 25km, but within a few minutes of setting off I and many of the other 25km runners veered off onto the ultra-marathon course due to poor signage! I only realised I'd gone wrong after about 18km – and we were very far from the finish. It was frustrating and disappointing. Eventually, I reached the finish after running 37km. After drinking a hot chocolate and resting up, I decided to put aside my frustrations. Instead, I was thankful that this detour was actually great preparation for a marathon I was doing four months later.

In a half marathon a few years ago, the lead bike took us off the course and down a little side street. A passer-by started shouting at the bike driver that we'd gone wrong, but the driver wasn't convinced. The two of them had a long conversation while us runners wondered where we were off to next. Eventually the passer-by steered us back onto the correct course and we were off again. In the distance we could see the rest of the field whizzing by on the correct course. My frustration was mixed with laughter; it felt like we were in a comedy film. It was certainly a brilliant opportunity to practise handling unexpected happenings!

Footwear can also be a common source of frustration. A practical piece of advice that I always give to runners is this: if you are lucky enough to find a model of trainers that you love and that fit beautifully, buy two or three pairs and keep them in reserve for future use. Shoe manufacturers change and update their models slightly year-by-year, so the exact shoe that you love might not be available again. The same model probably will be but it may have changed from the version you previously wore. It's far better to stock up than feel frustrated about your favourite shoe no longer being available when you return to buy another pair.

Staying in team accommodation for major competitions is something I often found stressful and not at all conducive to delivering my absolute best in a race. I rarely got enough sleep and rest, there was often noise and commotion going on and travel to meals and training locations was often time-consuming and tiring. I guess I am an introvert and like to have a quiet environment for resting and sleep. Therefore, an Athletes' Village full of thousands of athletes and staff – while exciting – was also challenging. The marathons are often held on the final day of championships, which means you have a long stay in this environment. Other athletes who have finished competing may be out celebrating as you need to rest for your race. Marathons are occasionally held on the first day and that is an absolute blessing. I took measures to improve things, like blacking out windows, taking my own snacks and being well organised. But this only works up to a point.

For the Osaka World Championships and Beijing Olympics, I asked for special permission to stay elsewhere. Thankfully, I was allowed to do this as an exception and it was an enormous and welcome relief. I knew I could go to sleep when I needed to, would not be bothered by noise, and could plan the days before my race to ensure I did everything I needed to do to prepare. Most importantly, it reduced the anxiety about staying in an environment which I knew I found stressful and over which I had little control. If I had been attending an event for which preparation was not critical, a noisy environment wouldn't have bothered me. But for a World Championships or Olympics that you have spent years preparing for you don't want any avoidable nuisance or trouble to detract from your performance. Years of hard work is a lot to throw down the drain because you have been kept up at night by noise. I decided it simply wasn't worth taking the risk.

Coping with training when you feel ropey is a challenge all runners face from time to time. Even if you do your best to look after yourself and recover between training sessions, sometimes for inexplicable reasons you simply don't feel up to training. In these circumstances, I always tried to accept the situation and adapt my training quickly. This could mean running the same session but reduced in volume; switching a speed session to an easy run; cross-training instead of running; or delaying a session until the next day. Usually, this resolved the problem quickly and I soon returned to my normal routine. By adapting and moving on, I limited the time I spent worrying about not feeling up to training.

When a situation is not to your liking, quickly changing your approach can bring a simple and positive solution.

Insight 42
Embrace Failure

Sport, especially elite sport, is all about striving, aiming high and pursuing goals. Some aspects of sport are not like this – for many people it's about seeing your friends, being out in the fresh air or enjoying non-competitive exercise. But so much of sport that we see around us, in elite competition coverage, advertising and even recreational sport, is about trying to be better.

This is all well and good, in some ways. It helps us to learn new skills and aspire to lofty goals; it inspires children and others to take up sports; and it provides role models for others to follow. Humans are evolved to be active. Sport and exercise are such a fundamental and huge part of our existence. When a cricketer successfully pulls off an unfeasibly difficult catch, a runner breaks a world record, or an ice skater achieves a perfect 10 score, we are enthralled by how they do these superhuman, dazzling things.

Yet, striving ever upwards – in other words, perfectionism – is not always positive by any means. Along with celebrating the very best come plenty of downsides. For example: the notion that anything less than the best is somehow not good enough; the enormous effort needed to constantly deliver the mental and physical exertion required to produce the best; the cruel judgments armchair athletes make about those who they deem to be sub-standard; and expecting superlative performances from athletes who have not been prepared accordingly to deliver. For aspiring elite athletes, this kind of environment can be like a pressure cooker. If you add social media into the mix, it's even worse – not only do you have to be brilliant at your sport, but you must have many followers and look like a million dollars at all times. It really is no wonder that eating disorders, mental ill-health and similar problems seem to be common, certainly in elite sport.

I am definitely guilty of perfectionism. I pushed myself relentlessly, yet was often not satisfied with how I ran in training and in races. I was always looking for something more. Perfectionism is often spoken about in negative terms; it is not something people talk about as a positive attribute. It's easy to criticise people who seem to be perfectionists. But nobody is born a perfectionist. It's a result of the environment you grow up and spend your life in, especially as a young person. The environments I have lived in at various stages of my life have certainly contributed to my perfectionism. This situation is not healthy by any means. While I was competing it was an uneasy treadmill that kept me going – the urge to always be better spurred me on to give my all and aim high. But the years since retiring I can only describe as disastrous for my mental health and confidence. My entire self-worth and identity were wrapped up with running fast. Elite athletes are often driven and focused individuals – they have to be, it's in the nature of the job – but because of that, they suffer when their vocation in sport is over. The transition from being a perfectionist elite athlete to an ordinary person needs great care.

Now I have lived a few more years since retiring, I can appreciate more how unhealthy a perfectionist outlook is. It may push you to achieve excellence, but it is difficult to sustain in the long term. I really fear for young people who show signs of perfectionism. My advice is what I discussed in Insight 28 – you must develop the ability to honestly and objectively assess yourself. Otherwise, you're at the mercy of other people's comments and always at risk of the perils of perfectionism.

The flipside of perfectionism is embracing failure – something that can be immensely valuable. Many of us don't do enough of it these days. Failing, or making mistakes, is a terrific way to learn. There is nothing inherently wrong with failing at something if you have genuinely and in good faith done your best to prepare. It's the unforgiving comments from others that often make people, especially young people, fearful of failure.

Now that I have retired but continue to run, I have adjusted my relationship with failure out of necessity. Gone are the days when I always aspired to go faster and break personal bests. It has not been easy to arrive at this point. I spent a fair while in denial, unable to properly say goodbye to my previous self and believing that I could return to elite level. On the plus side, failing to come out of retirement successfully forced me out of the denial phase and into acceptance, uncomfortable though it is. I have recalibrated what I can realistically hope for. Conversations with other runners of a similar age about re-setting goals, letting go of what you achieved when much younger and always looking forward have been so helpful.

Outings at Bushy Park parkrun are my staple these days, and it's a roller coaster of reluctantly embracing failure. In August 2018 to mark my 45th birthday and arrival in a new age group, I promised myself I would break 19 minutes. Considering that my marathon personal best of 2:23:12 calls for 5km splits of inside 17 minutes, 19 minutes was a modest aim. I ran 19:03. I had a self-talk and decided this was acceptable; I would try again the following week. I ran 19:03. The following week 19:03 again. I accepted that 19 minutes had defeated me and gave up. On other occasions I have been thrashed by small children, elderly men and a young father pushing two children in a twin buggy. On another outing following a foot injury, I set myself the goal of 20 minutes. Approaching the finish, I knew I had achieved it and felt happy. But I discovered I was so far down the field that I had failed for the first time ever to make it into the first finish funnel. And so it goes. Failure and I go along together in an uncomfortable embrace. I don't like it, but accept that it is a great way to learn.

> **Perfectionism is a mixed blessing. It is much healthier to embrace and learn from failure.**

Enjoy the Journey!

Thank you for reading my 42 insights from marathon running and for reaching this point. We are now into the final stretch, that magical last 195 metres to the finish. At this stage in a marathon, you can usually see the finish. You will be running past the finish line stands, noisy crowds and press cameras. All the hard work is done, there is a relatively tiny amount left to run, and you know the pain will be gone very soon ... unless you are unfortunate enough to be involved in a sprint finish, in which case a whole world of pain will be getting underway! Marathons and sprint finishes are never good bedfellows.

What is there left to say? I have explained all the key insights I learned as an elite marathon runner and from other parts of my running life. I have touched on all the important aspects of marathon running: training; nutrition; hydration; dealing with injuries; food; rest and recovery; preparing for racing; building mental strength; coping with setbacks; and more.

The central point I want to conclude this book with is perhaps the most important insight of all – to enjoy the journey. There is so much that we can enjoy about running, including: making lifelong friendships; training with your buddies; breaking a personal best; immersing yourself in beautiful environments; comparing notes on your Strava segments; inspiring children; doing something you thought was impossible; feeling physically fit; having a routine in your life; earning a piece of chocolate cake or a glass of wine ... the list is endless. It is a fabulous, simple and inexpensive sport that offers something to people of all levels and backgrounds. Yet, it's easy to get bogged down in the minutiae of hitting split times, feeling dissatisfied with what you have not achieved, gadgets being a nuisance, and so much more. This is the same as anything in life – it's easy to focus on what is frustrating and disappointing rather than the positive bits.

As with many, perhaps all the insights in this book, my own performance is by no means top-notch. I have a tendency to see the downsides, allow negative factors to affect me unduly, and fall into ruts of feeling low for a long time. I have now fully accepted and acknowledged this, and learned that finding positives and enjoyment in anything, however small, really is worth working at. Enjoying the journey every day, instead of simply driving forward full tilt at the destination – in other words, living your life in the moment – is paramount. I have to keep reminding myself of this every day. Forget about what might or might not be coming weeks, months or years down the track; let us concentrate on now and appreciate it. Good things can come to an abrupt end quickly and before you know it, something really special will be over. So, enjoy it while it lasts.

The last 195 metres of a marathon is a funny old world. Your legs are on the verge of, or may already be, buckling under you. There is a sense that if you stop running, you will never get going again. However tough it is, you simply have to keep running. You know that rest is coming but you have to push through the pain. If you are really unfortunate you may be suffering with an injury, willing a disappointing experience to end. But it's also a wonderful place to be and to journey through. Nearly all the suffering is behind you and done. Crowds will be cheering you on. The fruits of your labours over many months, years even, are reaped. You might be heading for a personal best or other major achievement. At any rate, if you have come this far, you will definitely finish. You will soon be celebrating or at the very least having a well-earned rest. It's fleeting and short-lived – under a minute for some runners and a few minutes at most for others. But you experience so much in that brief period of time. It's a whirlwind of physical and mental energy. If you haven't tried this particular 195 metre journey, I strongly recommend you have a go and more than once – in my experience, marathon racing gets better after the first time.

I hope you have enjoyed this distillation of what I learned as a runner. Of course, it is by no means everything there is to know about distance running. It's my experience. I hope very much that it has been useful and you can use these insights in your own life. Many of them apply to other aspects of our lives as much as they do to running.

Humans, or their ancestors, have been running for more than three million years. We will continue to run, way into the future. Running is an innate and integral part of the human condition. I am only one person among millions who happened to discover running, do it a lot and enjoy it. Each of us experiences it slightly differently, in our own unique way. This book explains mine. I wish you well on your running journey. Thank you for coming on my journey with me.

Congratulations and celebrations!

About the Author

Mara Yamauchi is one of the UK's fastest female marathon runners ever; a Commonwealth Games 10,000m bronze-medallist; and London Marathon runner-up. Her sixth-place finish in the 2008 Beijing Olympic Games is the joint best-ever performance by a British woman in the Olympic marathon.

An Oxford University graduate, she worked for 10 years for the Foreign and Commonwealth Office, has lived for many years in Kenya and Japan, and speaks Japanese.

A relative latecomer to running, she began serious training at age 18. Her elite career started with cross country and she was the English National Champion in 1998. She became a full-time athlete in her early thirties and competed at world level specialising in the marathon for eight years. In 2009, she was ranked second in the world in women's road running.

Mara retired from elite competition in 2013, suffered from mental ill-health after retiring and was divorced from her husband Shige in 2016. She lives in London, coaching running, commentating globally, as well as writing for her sport and mentoring other people to achieve their goals.

Mara Yamauchi Biography

1973:	Born in Oxford, UK
1973 – 1982:	Lived in Nairobi, Kenya; attended Kestrel Manor School
1982 – 1991:	Lived in Oxford, UK; attended Oxford High School GDST; ran with Radley Ladies AC then Headington Road Runners
1991 – 1992:	Gap year; travel to India and Israel; worked in Switzerland
1992 – 1995:	Studied for bachelor's degree in Politics, Philosophy and Economics at St. Anne's College, Oxford; trained with Oxford University Cross Country Club

1995 – 1996:   Studied for master's degree in Politics of the World Economy, London School of Economics; trained with Bob & Sylvia Parker at Parkside

1996 – 1997:   Joined Foreign Office, desk officer for Hungary and Slovakia

1997 – 1998:   Studied Japanese full-time; won English National Cross Country Championships; 38th in European Cross Country Championships

1998 – 1999:   Studied Japanese full-time at British Embassy Language School, Kamakura, Japan

1999 – 2002:   Worked at British Embassy, Tokyo, Political Section; returned to London

2003:   Head of Japan Section, FCO (job-share)

2004 – 2006:   Head of Diversity Team, HR Dept., FCO (job-share, then alone 70% time); London Marathon 2004 (first marathon, 2:39:16); 27th in World Cross Country Championships 2005; 18th and team bronze medal in World Athletics Championships Marathon 2005 (2:31:26); 5th in Tokyo International Women's Marathon 2005 (2:27:38)

2006 – 2011:   Lived in Tokyo as full-time athlete; 3rd in Kagawa Marugame International Half Marathon 2006 (69:24); won Ohme Road Race 10km 2006 (31:43); bronze medal in Commonwealth Games 10,000m 2006 (31:49); 23rd in World Cross Country Championships 2006; 6th in London Marathon 2006 (2:25:13); 6th in London Marathon 2007 (2:25:41); 2nd in Sapporo International Half Marathon 2007 (68:45); 9th in World Athletics Championships Marathon 2007 (2:32:55); won Osaka International Women's Marathon 2008 (2:25:10); 6th in Beijing Olympics Women's Marathon 2008 (2:27:29); 3rd in Tokyo International Women's Marathon 2008 (2:25:03); won Kagawa Marugame International Half Marathon 2009 (68:29), 2nd in London Marathon 2009 (2:23:12); won Ohme Road Race 30km 2010 (1:43:24); won New York City Half Marathon 2010 (69:25); 6th in London Marathon 2010 (2:26:16); 13th in New York City Marathon 2010 (2:31:38)

| 2011 – 2013: | Lived in Teddington, UK; 3rd in Yokohama Women's Marathon 2011 (2:27:24); London Olympics Women's Marathon 2012 (did not finish); retired 2013 |
| 2013: | Returned to and left FCO; qualified as Athletics coach; started self-employment as coach, speaker and writer. |

Contact the Author

Mara's website is www.marayamauchi.com

Twitter: @mara_yamauchi

Instagram: @mara_yamauchi

LinkedIn: @Mara Yamauchi

Photos Featured